Joan Gibson
from ♡ **W9-BVF-468**
Christmas 1982

The Pattern Library
CROCHET

The Pattern Library
CROCHET

Editor
Amy Carroll

Contributor
Dorothea Hall

BALLANTINE BOOKS · NEW YORK

First published in Great Britain in 1981 by
Ebury Press, National Magazine House,
72 Broadwick Street, London W1V 2BP

The Pattern Library CROCHET was conceived, edited
and designed by Dorling Kindersley Limited,
9 Henrietta Street, London WC2

Copyright © 1981 by Dorling Kindersley Limited

All rights reserved. No part of this publication may be reproduced, stored
in a retrieval system or transmitted in any form or by any means, electronic,
mechanical, photocopying, recording or otherwise, without the prior permission of
the copyright owner. Published in the United States by Ballantine Books, a division of
Random House, Inc., New York, and simultaneously in Canada by Random House
of Canada, Limited, Toronto, Canada.

Library of Congress Catalog Card Number: 81–66170

ISBN 0–345–29597–8

Manufactured in the United States of America

First Ballantine Books Edition: October 1981
10 9 8 7 6 5 4 3 2 1

Contents

Introduction

Crochet is an immensely satisfying craft. It is simple
and quick to work and, like knitting, is practical
and portable and has become an extremely popular
pastime. Throughout history crochet has been closely
associated with knitting, so much so that it was
not surprising that, with the introduction of many machine-
washable knitting yarns, an interest in all forms of
crochet was also revived.

Today, there are many specially-produced crochet
yarns available ranging from the very finest cotton – in
plain and random-dyed colors, shimmery lurex and glistening
bead-like threads – to thick chunky yarns.

The origins of crochet-stitch patterns are obscure but
crochet and other wool crafts have been practiced in
the Middle East for thousands of years. Over the
Renaissance period crochet patterns developed in imitation
of Guipure and Richelieu laces and needlepoint embroidery,
introducing, for example, single motifs tied with picot bars.
This technique was fully developed by crochet workers in
Ireland – from Cork in the south to Monaghan in the
north. The Irish introduced to their crochet rural motifs
such as farmyard animals, the wheel, rose and shamrock.

Some time later it was discovered that crochet
could be worked into a complete fabric and not be
restricted to lacy edgings and insertions.

Stitch patterns in this book include flat, ridged and raised
fabric stitches, textured puffball and loop stitches,
with information for working traditional Irish net patterns,
Afghan crochet and edgings, and many more, with
present-day techniques for working
medallions and colorwork patterns.

The aim throughout is to guide the crocheter through
all the techniques and to give a new dimension to the
ways in which these crochet stitch patterns
can be applied and extended.

All you need to begin to explore the myriad possibilities
of crochet are a hook and yarn. With these the
door is open to making many beautiful
things for your family and home.

BASIC TECHNIQUE

HOOKS

Crochet hooks are machine-made, usually from plastic-coated aluminum or steel. They are made in a range of sizes, conforming to the International Standard Range (ISR), from 14, for fine cottons, to 10, for working very thick rug yarn. Since the hooks do not hold stitches but hold only the working loop, they are all made to a standard length. Afghan crochet hooks are also available in metric sizes but are made in varying lengths to accommodate the correct number of stitches required.

WHICH YARN?

Choose the most appropriate yarn, hook and stitch pattern to suit your special needs. Generally, very fine yarns and hooks are used for delicate lacy effects, medium-weights for more practical fabrics, heavy-weights for warmth and hard-wearing qualities.

YARNS

In addition to a very wide range of specially-produced crochet threads, most yarns that are manufactured for knitting, knotting and weaving can be used.

Yarn describes any thread spun from natural fibers such as wool, cotton, linen, silk, or synthetics. **Ply** indicates the number of spun single threads which have been twisted together to produce a specific yarn. Single threads may be spun to any thickness so that ply does not refer to a standard thickness of yarn, although the terms 2-, 3- and 4-ply are often used to describe yarns of a recognized thickness. For instance, we might say that a particular spinner's yarn will "knit-up" to a 4-ply weight.

fine cotton

medium cotton

crêpe cotton

soft knitting cottons

macramé string

parcel string

jute

raffia

rayon

lurex

fine knitting yarn

medium knitting yarn

novelty mix

chunky yarn

rug wool

THE FOUNDATION CHAIN

To begin crochet, a slip knot is placed on the hook. This is a working loop and is never counted as a stitch. Stitches are made by pulling one loop through another to form a foundation chain upon which the next row or round is worked.

CHAIN STITCH (ch)

1 Hold back with slip knot in RH, twist hook under and over yarn.

2 Draw yarn through slip knot on hook.

A length of chain sts.

DOUBLE CHAIN STITCH (dch)

1 Make slip knot and work 2 ch, insert hook into 1st ch, yarn around hook (yo), draw loop through.

2 Yarn around hook, draw through both loops on hook. Repeat steps 1 and 2.

Use dchs for firm edge.

FINISHING OFF

1 Complete final st and cut yarn about 6 in. from work. Pull through last loop and tighten.

2 Thread loose end into yarn needle and darn into back of work.

COUNTING

Count dc as above. In doubles count 1 upright as 1 st. Count 1 ch between 2 dc as 3 sts.

TURNING CHAINS (t-ch)

Extra chains are worked at the end of a row before turning to bring the hook to the correct depth of the stitch being worked, so that the first stitch can be made evenly.

Table giving number of turning chains required for each stitch

single crochet: 1 turning chain
half double: 2 turning chains
double: 3 turning chains
treble: 4 turning chains
double treble: 5 turning chains

BASIC STITCHES

Each stitch gives a different texture and varies in depth, and every row makes a new chain line into which the next row is worked. Where stitches are worked back and forth in rows there is no right or wrong side to the fabric. *Note :* turning chain (**t-ch**) forms first stitch in row.

SLIP STITCH (sl st)

1 *Make no. of ch. Insert hook from F to B into 2nd ch from hook.*

2 *Yo, draw through 2 loops on hook. Repeat steps 1 and 2 to end.*

3 *Make 1 t-ch, turn, insert hook into B of first st of last row.*

SINGLE CROCHET (sc)

1 *Make ch row. Insert hook into 2nd ch from hook, yo, draw through.*

2 *Yo, draw through 2 loops. Repeat steps 1 and 2 to end.*

3 *1 t-ch, turn, insert hook under both loops of 1st st of last row.*

HALF DOUBLE (hdc)

1 *Make ch row. Yo and insert into 3rd ch, yo, draw through.*

2 *Yo, draw through 3 loops. Cont working hdc into every ch to end.*

3 *2 t-chs, turn. Make 1 hdc into 1st st of last row, rep to end.*

DOUBLE (dc)

1 *Make ch row. Yo, insert into 5th ch, yo, draw 1 loop through.*

2 *Yo, draw through first 2 lps on hook, rep one more.*

3 *Cont to end, 3 t-ch, turn. Make 1 tr into 2nd st of last row.*

9

TREBLE (tr)

1 *Make ch row. Yo twice, insert into 6th ch from hook, yo, draw lp through.*

2 *Yo and draw through first 2 lps on hook. Rep step 2 twice more.*

3 *Cont to end, make 4 t-ch, turn. Make first tr into 2nd st of row below.*

DOUBLE TREBLE (dtr)

1 *Make ch row. Yo 3 times, insert into 7th ch from hook, yo, draw loop through.*

2 *Yo and draw through first 2 lps on hook. Rep this step 3 times more.*

3 *Cont to end, make 5 t-ch, turn. Make first dtr into 2nd st of row below.*

SEAMS AND EDGES

Crochet sections may be joined together by sewing, using a blunt-ended wool needle with matching yarn, and a back stitch or woven seam as appropriate. You can also use single crochet; this gives a very firm seam and is often worked as an edging in a contrasting color on the right side of the fabric. Make sure that patterns such as stripes, shells or clusters match exactly before sewing.

Back stitch *For a firm seam, place pieces RS tog and pin. Backstitch evenly between crochet stitches.*

Woven seam *For a flat seam, place pieces WS up, edges touching. Weave needle loosely around both edge sts.*

Single crochet *For decorating edges, simply insert hook one st in from edge, work sc evenly through sts.*

BASIC STITCH VARIATIONS

Interesting variations to the basic stitches are made by inserting the hook into different parts of the stitch below and twisting the yarn in different ways.

Crossed single crochet
Work as for sc but take hook over yarn and draw loop through.

Working into half of stitch below
For RS ridge, insert hook into back of st in row below; into front of st for WS ridge.

Working between stitches
Insert hook into space between 2 sts in row below.

Working into stitches 2 rows below
Insert hook front to back between 2 sts, 2 rows below.

Working into chain space
Insert hook into space between ch sts in row below.

Working a raised effect
Insert hook from front around st below. For indented effect, insert hook from back.

TEXTURED STITCHES

Textures are created by working into the same stitch several times, as in bobble patterns, or by wrapping the yarn around the hook several times before drawing through, as in bullion stitch.

Bobble stitch
5 dc into next st, withdraw hook, insert into 1st dc, pick up lp, draw through.

Bullion stitch
Yo several times, insert hook into ch, yo, draw through, yo, draw through all loops.

Cabling around stitch
Yo, insert hook from back to front around dc in row below, work 1 dc.

LOOP STITCH

1 *Wrap yarn around L forefinger, insert hook into first st, catch both strands.*

2 *Draw 2 lps through drop lp from finger, yo. Draw through 3 lps on hook.*

3 *Rep steps 1 and 2 to end. Work 1 row sc before next lp row.*

OPENWORK STITCHES

Openwork mesh patterns are formed by missing stitches and working chains over the spaces left; the simplest way to make lacy crochet. Various patterns can be made by altering the combination of stitches and spaces.

Simple openwork
Work 1 dc, 2 ch, miss 2 ch in previous row, 1 dc into next ch. Rep to end.

Bar and lattice
1 dc, 3 ch, miss 2 ch in row below, 1 sc into next ch, 3 ch, miss 2 ch. Rep to end.

Simple net ground
Work 1 sc into 5th ch of row below, 5 ch, rep to end.

ADDING NEW YARN

Use these methods for joining in a new yarn or color. In small color patterns yarn not in use is carried along top of row below until required. Vertical or diagonal stripes require a ball of yarn for each color; twist once as new color is picked up.

New yarn in sc
1 *Run new yarn along top of previous row, work over it as if part of row below. When needed introduce with last yo of sc.*

2 *If old yarn is reqd again in row carry along as step 1. If not, cut off after few sts. Leave at back if reqd in same place next row.*

NEW YARN IN DC

1 *Carry new yarn along top of previous row until required. Yo with old yarn, insert hook.*

2 *Yo with both yarns, draw through. Yo with new yarn and complete dc.*

3 *Carry old yarn along top of previous row until reqd. If not, cut off after a few sts.*

WORKING IN THE ROUND

Circular crochet is worked continuously around a central point starting with a foundation ring. The crochet can either be worked as a flat medallion, shaped as a beret or as a tube. Where a small number of chains are required use a ring of slip stitches. Where a large number of chains are required use a ring of single crochet.

1 *Make a circle with yarn as shown. Insert hook, yo, draw through circle, yo, draw through loop.*

2 *Work required number of sc around circle and over both strands.*

3 *Pull loose end firmly to draw circle together. Close ring with a slip stitch.*

AFGHAN CROCHET

Afghan crochet is worked with a number of stitches carried on a single hook. The stitches are worked from a foundation row of chains. Stitches for the first row are picked up working from right to left. Then, on the second row, working from left to right, stitches are made and discarded without turning the work around.

1 *Working from R to L, insert hook into ch, yo, draw lp through. Cont to end.*

2 *Working from L to R, yo, draw through 1st lp, *yo, draw through 2 lps, rep from * to end.*

3 *For all R to L rows, insert hook through vertical lp of st below. Rep steps 1 and 2.*

INCREASING (inc)

Crochet will become wider by increasing the number of stitches in a row or round. The simplest method is to work extra stitches into the same stitch either at the beginning, at both ends, or in the middle of a row, as a single or double increase.

Single increase at each end of row
Work twice into first or last st.

Single increase in middle of row
Work twice into any st. Mark st with contrast yarn.

Double increases
Work 3 times into same st on previous row.

MULTIPLE INCREASES

Several stitches may be increased at the edge of the work by making extra chain stitches.

Adding stitches at beginning of row
Make same no. of extra ch as sts reqd plus t-chs, turn. Work new sts in pattern.

Adding stitches at end of row
To keep increases made at both ends of row level make provision for these stitches on previous row.
1 *Make same no. of extra ch as sts reqd plus t-chs. Work sl st over new ch, cont in pattern.*

2 *On next row, continue to end in pattern working through slip stitches.*

DECREASING (dec)

Crochet will become narrower by decreasing the number of stitches in a row. The simplest method is to miss a stitch either at the beginning, the middle or the end of a row. Alternative methods are; to decrease at the edge by leaving stitches unworked or to work two stitches together as one.

Missing a stitch at each end of row
At beg, t-ch, miss 1st, work next st. At end, miss next to last st, work final st. For double dec, miss 2 sts.

Decreasing several stitches at row ends
At beg, work sl st over reqd dec sts, make t-chs, cont in pattern. At end, leave reqd dec sts unworked, make t-chs.

Decreasing in middle of row
Work 2 sts tog as 1. As guide for further dec mark position of dec sts with colored yarn.

WORKING WITH TWO STITCHES AS ONE

In each case, use the method given below for decreasing in the middle or at the end of a row.

Single crochet
Make t-ch, insert hook into first st, yo, draw through. Rep into next st, yo, draw through all lps.

Double
Make 3 t-ch, yo, insert hook into first st, draw through, yo, draw through 2 lps. Rep into next st, yo, draw through all lps.

Half double
Make 2 t-ch. Yo, insert hook into first st, yo, draw through. Rep into next st, yo, draw through all lps.

PUTTING THE STITCH PATTERNS TO USE

Before you begin any crochet work make a tension sample first. This is necessary whether you wish to check your tension measurements against a printed pattern, substitute the suggested stitch or yarn with another, or create a new design.

Making a tension sample
Work a test piece slightly larger than 4 in. square. Lay on a flat surface and mark out the tension measurement given in pattern with pins. Count the rows and stitches between pins. If there are too many stitches between pins try a larger hook; if too few, try a smaller hook.

SUBSTITUTING ONE STITCH FOR ANOTHER

Make sure that your substitute stitch is of a similar type to the one suggested in the pattern, and that the stitch multiple will divide evenly into the foundation chain. Stitch multiples in crochet are generally small and can usually be adjusted at the tension sample stage. You may also substitute one yarn for another, providing you choose one from the same group as the original, eg. fine cotton or knitting worsted yarn, working a tension sample first.

HOOK AND YARN TABLE

14	very fine cotton	F	medium-weight
12		G	knitting worsted
10		H	yarn
7	fine cotton and	I	double crêpe,
4	equivalent yarns		mohair
0			
		K	Aran-type
B	light-weight yarns	L	double, double yarn
C			
E		M	chunky,
		N	heavy-weight

ABBREVIATIONS

alt	alternate(ly)	**no.**	number
B	back	**patt**	pattern
beg	begin(ning)	**pc**	picot
bet	between	**RDF**	round double front
ch(s)	chain(s)	**rem**	remain(ing)
cl	cluster	**rep**	repeat
col	colour	**reqd**	required
cont	continu(e)(ing)	**rnd**	round
dec	decreas(e)(ing)	**RS**	right side
dc	double crochet	**sc**	single crochet
dch(s)	double chain(s)	**sl st**	slip stitch
dtr	double treble	**sp(s)**	spare(s)
F	front	**st(s)**	stitch(es)
foll	follow(ing)	**tog**	together
gr(s)	group(s)	**tr**	treble
hdc	half double	**tr tr**	triple treble
inc	increas(e)(ing)	**t-ch(s)**	turning chain(s)
lp(s)	loop(s)	**WS**	wrong side
		yo	yarn around hook

Symbols

A star * shown in a pattern row denotes that the stitches shown after this sign must be repeated from that point.

Round brackets ( ), enclosing a particular stitch combination, denote that the stitch combination must be repeated in the order shown.

Hyphens refer to those stitches which have already been made but which will be used as the base for the next stitch, eg., you would work 2tr into 2-ch sp, by making 2 trebles into the space created by the chain stitches worked in the previous row.

BASIC STITCH PATTERNS

*A few simple stitches form the basis of all
crochet stitch patterns producing a flat surface
and firm fabric (see p.9). Variations to these basic
stitches are numerous and include basketweave,
cable, ridged and raised effects (see p.11).*

Double stitch

Materials Fine rayon or random-dyed yarn for spring wear;
medium or heavy-weight wool for a warm, dense-textured fabric.
Uses All-over pattern for waistcoat front, baby's jacket or blanket
border; coat or sweater inset panel.

Make any number of ch, 1ch,
turn.
Row 1 Insert hook into 2nd ch
from hook, yo, draw lp through,
insert hook into next ch, yo,
draw lp through, yo, draw
through all 3 lps on hook, ★ insert
hook into same ch as 2nd lp of
previous st, yo, draw lp through,
insert hook into next ch, yo,
draw lp through, yo, draw
through all 3 lps on hook, rep
from ★ to end, 1sc into last st,
1ch, turn.

Row 2 Insert hook into first st,
yo, draw lp through, insert hook
into next st, yo, draw lp through,
yo, draw through all 3 lps on
hook, ★ insert hook into same st as
2nd lp of previous st, yo, draw lp
through, insert hook into next st,
yo, draw lp through, yo, draw
through all 3 lps on hook, rep
from ★ to end, 1sc into last st,
1ch, turn.
Rep row 2 throughout.

Spider stitch

Materials Fine to medium-weight yarn for a pretty, summery look.

Uses Dress yoke or cardigan inset panel; all-over repeat for baby's carriage set or small purse.

Make an even number of ch, 2ch, turn.

Row 1 (1sc, 1ch, 1sc) into 3rd ch from hook, ★ miss 1ch, (1sc, 1ch, 1sc) into next ch, rep from ★ to last ch, 1sc into last ch, 2ch, turn.

Row 2 ★ (1sc, 1ch, 1sc) into ch sp, rep from ★ to end, 1sc into t-ch, 2ch, turn.

Rep row 2 throughout.

Ridged doubles

Materials Chunky or knitting worsted yarn for a sporty look; medium-weight cotton or lurex for special evening wear.

Uses Sweater inset panel or child's jacket and matching cap; dress yoke or nightie bodice for purchased fabric skirt.

These are also called *stand doubles*. Make any number of ch, 3ch, turn.

Work a row of dc on foundation ch, 3ch, turn.

Row 1 ★ 1dc into next st, inserting hook through back half only of st, rep from ★ to end, 3ch, turn.

Rep row 1 throughout.

Ridge stitch

Materials Lightly twisted cotton or synthetic yarn for easy care; chunky or medium yarn for a firm, nubbly fabric.
Uses All-over repeat for beach outfit, bathroom set, cushion or placemat; jacket or dress inset panel.

Make any number of ch, 1ch, turn.
Work a row of sc on foundation ch, 1ch, turn.
Row 1 * 1sc into next sc, inserting hook through back half only of st, rep from * to end, 1ch, turn.
Rep row 1 throughout.

Cable stitch

Materials 2- to 4-ply wool for warmth; acrylic or silky yarn for party wear.
Uses Sweater yoke or baby's shawl panel; full-length coat inset band or all-over design for deep V-neck slipover.

Make a number of ch divisible by 4 plus 2, 1ch, turn.
Work a row of sc on foundation ch, 3ch, turn.
Row 1 * Miss next st, 1 dc into each of next 3 sts, yo, insert hook from front to back into the st which was missed and work a dc, rep from * to end, 1dc into t-ch, 1ch, turn.
Row 2 1sc into each st to end, 3ch, turn.
Rep rows 1 and 2 throughout.

Raised doubles

Materials Knitting worsted wool for warmth; fine to medium-weight yarn for a firm, ridged effect.

Uses Inset panel for father and son cardigan; all-over pattern for sweater, dress bodice or toddler's jacket.

Make an odd number of ch, 3ch, turn. Work a row of tr of foundation ch, 1ch, turn.

Row 1 1sc into each tr to end, 1sc into t-ch, 2ch, turn.

Row 2 * Yo, keeping hook at front of work, insert hook from right to left round stem of next dc on foundation row and work a dc – called RDF – miss sc above this dc, 1sc into next sc, rep from * to end, ending with 1RDF round stem of last dc, 1sc into t-ch, 1ch, turn.

Row 3 1sc into each st to end, 1sc into t-ch, 2ch, turn.

Row 4 * 1RDF round stem of RDF on row 2, 1sc into next sc, rep from * to end, working last sc into t-ch, 1ch, turn.

Rep rows 3 and 4 throughout.

Crossed half doubles

Materials Medium-weight yarn for a pretty textured look; Shetland or baby wool for softness.

Uses Sweater or blouson jacket inset panel; all-over design for mother and daughter slipover or baby's shawl.

Make an odd number of ch, 2ch, turn.

Row 1 Yo, insert hook into 3rd ch from hook, yo, draw lp through, yo, insert hook into next ch, yo, draw lp through, yo, draw through all 5 lps on hook, 1ch, * (yo, insert hook into next ch, yo, draw lp through) twice, yo, draw through all 5 lps on hook, 1ch, rep from * to last ch, 1hdc into last ch, 2ch, turn.

Row 2 Yo, insert hook into first ch sp, yo, draw lp through, yo, insert hook into next ch sp, yo, draw lp through, yo, draw through all 5 lps on hook, 1ch, * yo, insert hook into same ch sp as last lp of previous st, yo, draw lp through, yo, insert hook into next ch sp, yo, draw lp through, yo, draw through all 5 lps on hook, 1ch, rep from * to end, 1 hdc into t-ch, 2ch, turn.

Rep row 2 throughout.

Basket stitch

Materials Medium-weight wool or novelty mix for a classic look; random-dyed cotton for beach wear.

Uses Inset band or all-over pattern for button-through cardigan; all-over repeat for bikini or beach blanket border.

Make a number of ch divisible by 4 plus 3, 1ch, turn. Work a row of sc foundation ch, 1ch, turn.

Row 2 * 1sc into next sc, inserting hook through back half only of st, rep from * to end, 1ch, turn.

Row 3 1sc into back half of each of first 3sc, * insert hook into st below next sc (i.e. 1 row down) and work a sc, miss this sc, 1sc into back half of next 3sc, rep from * to end, 1ch, turn.

Row 4 1sc into back half of each st to end, 1ch, turn.

Row 5 1sc into back half of first sc, * 1sc into sc below next sc, miss this sc, 1sc into back half of next 3sc, rep from * to last 2 sts, 1sc into sc below next sc, 1sc into back half of last sc, 1ch, turn.

Row 6 As row 4.

Rep rows 3 to 6 throughout.

TEXTURED PATTERNS

Deeply-textured patterns are made by raising and lowering the fabric in such a way as to create a regular stitch repeat (see p.11). Repeat sizes may be small or large involving a single puffball or cluster; all-over loop, shell and honeycomb designs; or, groups of pineapples or tulips which can be arranged as borders, large spot repeats or all-over patterns.

Raised dots in pineapple stitch

Materials Fine cotton or synthetic yarn for wash and wear; Shetland wool for an Aran effect.

Uses All-over repeat for sleeveless pullover, baby's cot cover or beret; sweater or shawl inset panel.

Make a number of ch divisible by 4 plus 3, 1ch, turn.
Work 3 rows in sc, 1ch, turn.
Row 4 1sc into each of first 3 sts, ★ insert hook into next st, yo, draw lp through, (yo, insert hook into the same st 2 rows below – i.e. first row – yo, draw lp through, yo, draw through 2 lps) 6 times, yo, draw through all 8 lps on hook – called 1 pineapple – 1sc into each of next 3sc, rep from ★ to end, 1ch, turn.
Work 3 rows in sc, 1ch, turn.
Row 8 1sc into first sc, ★ 1 pineapple into next sc, 1sc into each of next 3sc, rep from ★ to last 2 sts, 1 pineapple into next sc, 1sc into next sc, 1ch, turn.
Rep rows 1 to 8 throughout.

Raised diagonal pineapple

Materials Medium-weight, cotton or acrylic for seaside holiday wear; knitting worsted wool for Arans.

Uses All-over design for loose-fitting slipover, bed set and bolster; poncho or sweater inset panel.

Make a number of ch divisible by 4 plus 3, 1ch, turn. Work 3 rows in sc, 1ch, turn.

Row 4 1sc into each of first 3 sts, * insert hook into next st, yo, draw lp through, (yo, insert hook into the same st 2 rows below – i.e. first row – yo, draw lp through, yo, draw through 2 lps) 6 times, yo, draw through all 8 lps on hook – called 1 pineapple – 1sc into each of next 3sc, rep from * to end, 1ch, turn. Work 3 rows in sc, 1ch, turn.

Row 8 2sc, * 1 pineapple, 3sc, rep from * to last st, 1 pineapple into last sc, 1ch, turn.

Work 3 rows in sc, 1ch, turn.

Row 12 1sc into first sc, * 1 pineapple into next sc, 1sc into each of next 3sc, rep from * to last 2 sts, 1 pineapple into next sc, 1sc into next sc, 1ch, turn.

Work 3 rows in sc, 1ch, turn.

Row 16 1 pineapple into next st, * 1sc into each of next 3sc, 1 pineapple into next sc, rep from * to last 2 sts, 1sc into each of next 2sc, 1ch, turn.

Rep rows 1 to 16 throughout.

Spray stitch

Materials Very fine cotton or silky yarn for special occasions; 2-ply wool for light warmth.

Uses Bridesmaid's purse, party dress insertion or necktie; baby's shawl inset panel, or all-over repeat for bride's cape.

Make a number of ch divisible by 3 plus 1, 2ch, turn.

Row 1 2dc into 3rd ch from hook, ★ skip 2ch, (1sc, 2dc) into next ch, rep from ★ to last 3ch, skip 2ch, 1sc into last ch, 2ch, turn.

Row 2 2dc into first sc, ★ (1sc, 2dc) into next sc, rep from ★ to end, 1sc into t-ch, 2ch, turn.

Rep row 2 throughout.

Tulip stitch

Materials Medium-weight wool, lurex, silk or rayon yarn for a party look; very fine crochet cotton for sheer daintiness.

Uses All-over pattern for an evening wrap, loose-fitting short waistcoat or pouch bag; edging for print shawl or braces.

Make a number of ch divisible by 4, plus 1, 3ch, turn.

Row 1 3dc into 4th ch from hook, ★ skip 3ch, (1sc, 3ch, 3dc) into next ch, rep from ★ to last 4ch, skip 3ch 1sc into last ch, 3ch, turn.

Row 2 3dc into first sc, ★ (1sc, 3ch, 3dc) into 3ch lp, rep from ★ to last lp, 1sc into last lp, 3ch, turn.

Raised puffballs

Materials Cotton or synthetic yarn for washability; chunky or knitting worsted wool for a sporty, Aran look.

Uses Cushion set or hooded blouson jacket; sweater or poncho inset panel; all-over design for bedspread.

Make a number of ch divisible by 6 plus 5, 1ch, turn. Work 3 rows in sc, 1ch, turn.

Row 4 1sc into each of next 5sc, ★ 1ch, (1dc into next st 2 rows below) 6 times (all into the same st), take hook out of last dc, insert it into the first ch of this grp, pull the lp of the dc through the ch – called puffball – skip this sc, 1sc into each of next 5sc, rep from ★ to end, 1ch, turn.

Work 3 rows in sc, 1ch, turn.

Row 8 1sc into each of first 2sc, ★ 1ch, 1 puffball below next sc, skip this sc, 1sc into each of next 5sc, rep from ★ to last 3 sts, 1 puff ball below next sc, 1sc into each of last 2sc, 1 ch, turn.

Rep rows 1 to 8 throughout.

Blossom stitch

Materials Medium-weight crochet cotton, rayon or fine wool for a close textured fabric.

Uses Cushion, blanket border or straw hat band; sweater or bed-jacket inset panel.

Make a number of ch divisible by 4 plus 3, 2ch, turn.

Row 1 (1dc, 1ch, 1dc) into 3rd ch from hook, skip 1ch, 1sc into next ch, ★ skip 1ch, (1dc, 1ch, 1dc) into next ch, skip 1ch, 1sc into next ch, rep from ★ to end, 2ch, turn.

Row 2 ★ 1dc into sc, 1ch, 1sc into ch sp, 1ch, rep from ★ to end, 1dc into t-ch, 2ch, turn.

Row 3 ★ (1dc, 1ch, 1dc) into sc, 1sc into dc, rep from ★ to end, working last sc into t-ch, 2ch, turn.

Rep rows 2 and 3 throughout.

Rope stitch

Materials Baby wool for softness; fine to medium-weight cotton, lurex or silky yarn for evening wear.
Uses All-over design for shawl or baby's cot cover; camisole top or overblouse inset panel.

Make a number of ch divisible by 3, 3ch, turn.
Row 1 1dc into 4th ch from hook, 1ch, 1dc into next ch, * skip 1ch, 1dc into next ch, 1ch, 1dc into next ch, rep from * to last ch, 1dc into last ch, 3ch, turn.
Row 2 (1dc, 1ch, 1dc) into each ch sp to end, 1dc into t-ch, 3ch, turn. Rep row 2 throughout.

Honeycomb stitch

Materials 3- to 4-ply wool or knitting worsted yarn, space-dyed acrylic or novelty mix for casual wear.

Uses Jacket or sweater inset panel or all-over repeat for slipover, beret or blanket square.

Make a number of ch divisible by 3, 1ch, turn.
Work a row of sc on foundation ch, 1ch, turn.

Row 1 * Yo, insert hook into next st, (yo, draw lp through, yo, draw through 2 lps) 5 times, yo, draw through 6 lps, 1sc into each of next 2sc, rep from * to end, 1ch, turn.

Row 2 1sc into each st to end, 1ch, turn.

Row 3 * 1sc into each of next 2sc, yo, insert hook into next st, (yo, draw lp through, yo, draw through 2 lps) 5 times, yo, draw through 6 lps, rep from * to end, 1ch, turn.

Row 4 As row 2.

Rep rows 1 to 4 throughout.

Paris stitch

Materials 3- to 4-ply cotton, crêpe or tweedy mix yarn for a classic look.

Uses Dress inset panel, blanket square or all-over pattern for twin-set.

Make a number of ch divisible by 3 plus 1, 3ch, turn.

Row 1 (1dc, 2ch, 1sc) into 4th ch from hook, * skip 2ch, (2dc, 2ch, 1sc) into next ch, rep from * to end, 3ch, turn.

Row 2 (1dc, 2ch, 1sc) into 2ch sp, * (2dc, 2ch, 1sc) into next 2ch sp, rep from * to end, 3ch, turn.

Rep row 2 throughout.

Sweetpea stitch

Materials Medium-weight crêpe-rayon, cotton, silk or acrylic yarn for a lacy effect.

Uses Inset panel for child's dress or baby's carriage set; all-over design for classic cardigan, sleeveless pullover or dress bodice.

Make a number of ch divisible by 7 plus 4, 3ch, turn.

Row 1 1dc into 4th ch from hook, * skip 2ch, 5dc into next ch, skip 2ch, 1dc into each of next 2ch, rep from * to last 3ch, skip 2ch, 3dc into last ch, 3ch, turn.

Row 2 1dc bet first 2dc, * 5dc bet the 2 single dc, 1dc bet 2nd and 3rd of 5dc, 1dc bet 3rd and 4th of 5dc, rep from * to end, 3dc bet last dc and t-ch, 3ch, turn.

Rep row 2 throughout.

Turtle stitch

Materials Silky yarn or cotton for a softly textured fabric; 3- or 4-ply wool for light warmth.
Uses All-over repeat for loose-fitting waistcoat, silky cravat, necktie or napkin ring; sweater yoke or bedjacket inset panel.

Make a number of ch divisible by 6 plus 4, ch, turn.
Row 1 3dc into 4th ch from hook, skip 2ch, 1sc into next ch, ★ skip 2ch, 5dc into next ch, skip 2ch, 1sc into next ch, rep from ★ to end, 3ch, turn.
Row 2 Working into the back half only of each st, 3dc into sc, ★ 1sc into 3rd of 5dc, 5dc into sc, rep from ★ to end, 1sc into t-ch, 3ch, turn.
Rep row 2 throughout.

Close shell stitch

Materials Cotton or silky yarn for summer wear; 3- to 4-ply yarn or baby wool for light-weight warmth.
Uses All-over design for dress bodice or loose waistcoat; inset panel for baby's jacket or toddler's dress.

Make a number of ch divisible by 6 plus 4, 3ch, turn.
Row 1 3dc into 4th ch from hook, skip 2ch, 1sc into next ch, ★ skip 2ch, 4dc into next ch, skip 2ch, 1sc into next ch, rep from ★ to end, 3ch, turn.
Row 2 2dc into sc, ★ 1sc bet 2nd and 3rd dc, 4dc into sc, rep from ★ to end, 1sc bet last dc and t-ch, 3ch, turn.
Rep row 2 throughout.

Parquet stitch

Materials Fine to medium-weight cotton or acrylic for wash and wear; lurex or silky yarn for a summery look.

Uses Bag inset panel, yoke band and shoulder ties for print dress; all-over design for slipover, ribbon-threaded evening purse or buffet runner.

Make a number of ch divisible by 3 plus 1, 1ch, turn.

Row 1 1sc into 2nd ch from hook, * 2ch, skip 2ch, 1sc into next ch, rep from * to end, 3ch, turn.

Row 2 1dc into first dc, * 3dc into next sc, rep from * to end, 2dc into last sc, 1ch, turn.

Row 3 1sc into first dc, * 2ch, 1sc into 2nd of 3dc, rep from * to end, 2ch, 1sc into t-ch, 3ch, turn.

Rep rows 2 and 3 throughout.

Loop stitch

Materials Cotton or synthetic yarn for easy care; 4-ply yarn, knitting worsted or chenille for warmth.

Uses Jacket trim or all-over pattern for bathroom set; all-over repeat for full-length coat and beret, egg or teapot cosy, pram cover or furry toys.

Make any number of ch, 1ch, turn. Work a row of sc on the foundation ch, 1ch, turn.

Row 1 (wrong side of work) * Yo, insert hook into next st, take yarn round finger, draw lp through, yo, draw through 3 lps on hook, rep from * to end, 1ch, turn.

Row 2 1sc into each st to end, 1ch, turn.

Rep rows 1 and 2 throughout.

COLOR PATTERNS

Many attractive and intricate effects can be crocheted simply by introducing two or more colors into patterns (see p.12). As the technique for working color patterns produces a close fabric, it is generally advisable to use a hook one size larger than the normal choice for the chosen yarn. Patterns vary from a single dot repeat through speckle and petal patterns to undulating peaks and pinnacles.

Dot stitch

Materials Fine to medium-weight yarn for a two-tone ermine effect.
Uses Front inset panel for classic twinset or all-over pattern for boy or girl sleeveless pullover, gloves or hat.

This pattern uses 2 colors, A and B.
Using A, make a number of ch divisible by 3 plus 1, 1ch, turn.
Row 1 1sc into 2nd ch from hook, * 2ch, skip 2ch, 1sc into next ch, rep from * to end, joining B on last sc.
Row 2 Using B, 4ch, * 3dc into 2ch sp, 1ch, rep from * to end, 1dc into last sc.

Row 3 Return to beg of row 2, draw A through under 4th of 4ch, 1ch as first sc, *2ch, 1sc into 1ch sp, rep from * to end, drawing B through on last sc.
Row 4 Using B, work as row 2. Always starting each row at the end where the correct color was left, rep rows 3 and 4 throughout.

Brick stitch

Materials Medium to heavy-weight yarn for a pebbly textured, warm fabric.

Uses Edge detail for knitted cardigan or all-over design for a toddler's first coat, family sweaters or cushion set.

This pattern uses 3 colors, A, B and C.

Using A, make a number of ch divisible by 4 plus 2, 2ch, turn.

Row 1 1dc into 4th ch from hook, *2ch, skip 2ch, 1dc into each of next 2ch, rep from * to end, joining in B on last dc.

Row 2 Using B, 2ch, *1dc into each of the 2 skipped ch on row 1, 2ch, rep from * to end, ending with 1ch instead of 2, then sl st into 3rd of 3ch at beg of row 1, joining in C.

Row 3 Using C, 3ch, 1dc into skipped dc on last row, *2ch, 1dc into each of 2 skipped dc on last row, rep from * to end, drawing A through on last dc.

Row 4 Using A, work as row 2. Working 1 row in each color throughout rep rows 3 and 4.

Almond stitch

Materials Chunky yarn for warmth; knitting worsted or tweedy mix for a sporty look.

Uses Jacket inset band; all-over pattern for lady's golf sweater or family slippers.

This stitch uses 2 colors, A and B.

Using A make a number of ch divisible by 10 plus 1, 1ch, turn.

Row 1 1sc into 2nd ch from hook 1sc into each ch to end, joining in B on last sc.

Row 2 Using B, 1ch, *1sc into next st, 1hdc into next sc, 1dc into each of next 5 sts, 1hdc into next st, 1sc into next st, 1ch, skip 1 st, rep from * to end, sl st into t-ch, turn.

Row 3 Using B, 1ch, *1sc into sc, 1hdc into hdc, 1dc into each of 5dc, 1hdc into hdc, 1sc into sc, 1ch, rep from * to end, sl st into t-ch, drawing A through.

Row 4 3ch, *1sc into each of next 9 sts, 1dc into skipped st of row 1, rep from * to end, ending with 1dc into t-ch.

Row 5 Using A, 1ch, 1sc into each st to end, drawing through B on last sc.

Row 6 Using B, 3ch, 1dc into each of next 2 sts, *1hdc into next st, 1sc into next st, 1ch, skip 1st, 1sc into next st, 1hdc into next st, 1dc into each of next 5 sts, rep from * to end, but ending with 3dc instead of 5.

Row 7 3ch, 1dc into each of next 2dc, *1hdc into hdc, 1sc into sc, 1ch, 1sc into sc, 1hdc into hdc, 1dc into each of 5dc, rep from * to end, but ending with 3dc instead of 5 and draw through A on last dc.

Row 8 Using A, 1ch as first sc, 1sc into each of next 4 sts, *1dc into skipped st of row 5, 1sc into each of next 9 sts, rep from * to end, but ending with 1sc into each of next 5 sts.

Row 9 As row 5.

Rep rows 2 to 9 throughout.

Pinnacle stitch

Materials Shetland, knitting worsted wool or mohair for warmth or for a figure-flattering fabric.

Uses All-over repeat for throwover bedspread, shaded cushion set or travel rug; dress or skirt, shawl or scarf border.

This pattern uses 2 colors, A and B.

Using A, make a number of ch divisible by 14 plus 1, 2ch, turn.

Row 1 1sc into 3rd ch from hook, *1sc into each of next 5ch, skip 3ch, 1sc into each of next 5ch, 3sc into next ch, rep from * to end, but ending with 2sc into last ch instead of 3.

Row 2 1ch, 1sc into same place, * 1sc into each of next 5sc, skip 2sc, 1sc into each of next 5sc, 3sc into next sc, rep from * to end, but ending with 2sc into t-ch. Rep row 2 throughout, working 2 more rows in A, then 4 rows in B and 4 rows in A throughout.

Petal stitch

Materials Medium-weight wool, silk, crêpe or acrylic yarn for softness; crochet cotton for a finer fabric.

Uses Dress yoke, slipover inset panel or all-over pattern for bedjacket or shawl; scatter cushion border, deep collar and cuffs or waistcoat trim.

This pattern uses 2 colors, A and B.

Using A make a number of ch divisible by 6 plus 1, 3ch, turn.

Row 1 2dc into 4th ch from hook, * skip 2ch, 1sc into next ch, skip 2ch, 5dc into next ch, rep from * to end, ending with 3dc into last ch instead of 5.

Row 2 Join B to top of 3ch at beg of row 1, 1sc into this st, *2ch, ** yo, insert hook into next dc, yo, draw lp through, yo, draw through 2 lps ** rep from ** to ** into next dc, into sc, then into each of next 2dc, yo, draw through 6 lps on hook, 2ch, 1sc into next sc, rep from * to end, drawing through A on last sc.

Row 3 Using A, 3ch, 2dc into first sc, *1sc into top of grp, 5dc into next sc, rep from * to end, but ending with 3dc into last sc.

Row 4 Return to beg of row 3, draw B through top of 3ch and work as row 2.

Rep rows 3 and 4 throughout.

Speckle stitch

Materials Medium-weight wool or synthetic yarn for a rich tweedy effect.

Uses Mother and daughter sweater inset panel or all-over pattern for man's sleeveless cardigan or deerstalker cap.

This pattern uses 3 colors, A, B and C.

Using A, make a number of ch divisible by 3 plus 2, 1ch, turn.

Row 1 1sc into 3rd ch from hook, 1sc into each ch to end.

Row 2 1ch, 1sc into each sc to end. Do not break off A.

Row 3 Join B, 1ch, 1sc into each sc to end.

Row 4 As row 2. Do not break off B.

Row 5 Return to beg of row 4, join in C, 1ch, 1sc into each sc to end. Do not break off C.

Row 6 Draw A through first st, 1ch, 1sc into next sc, *1tr inserting hook from right to left in front of corresponding st on row 2, 1sc into each of next 2sc, rep from * to end.

Row 7 As row 2.

Row 8 Draw C through first st, 1ch, 1sc into each sc to end.

Row 9 Return to beg of row 8, draw B through first st, 1ch, 1sc into next sc, *1tr, inserting hook from right to left in front of tr on row 6, 1sc into each of next 2sc, rep from * to end.

Row 10 As row 2.

Always starting each row at the correct end where yarn was left, rep rows 5 to 10 throughout.

OPENWORK

*Open work stitch patterns are some of the quickest
and easiest to crochet (see p.12). As all openwork is
made by leaving large spaces between stitches, the work
grows rapidly. This group of lacy stitch patterns,
combined with the variety of crochet yarns available,
offers one of the widest ranges of decorative
textures – from a simple net ground, arch,
picot and knot to intricate crown and
peacock patterns.*

Simple net ground

Materials Cotton for easy care; very fine wool, silk or lurex for special evening wear.

Uses All-over pattern for loose-fitting slipover or beach bag; shimmery shawl or dress and jacket inset panel.

Make a number of ch divisible by
4 plus 1, 5ch, turn.

Row 1 1sc into 10th ch from hook, * 5ch, skip 3ch, 1sc into next ch, rep from * to end, 5ch, turn.

Row 2 1sc into 5ch lp, * 5ch, 1sc into next lp, rep from * to end, 5ch, turn.
Rep row 2 throughout.

Solomon's knot

Materials Medium-weight dishcloth cotton, bouclé yarn or mohair for softness; fine string, tubular rayon or russia braid for furnishing.

Uses All-over pattern for curtain room divider, scarf or shawl; shopping bag, applied border for lampshade, woven bedspread or rug trim.

There is no foundation ch for this stitch. Make a slip knot and put onto hook.

Row 1 *Draw lp up to ½in., yo, draw lp through, insert hook bet double and single threads of lp just made, yo, draw lp through, yo, draw through both lps on hook, rep from * for length reqd, making an even no. of knots, turn.

Row 2 Skip knot on hook and next 3 knots, work 1sc into next knot, * make 2 knots as on row 1, skip 1 knot on row 1, work 1sc into next knot, rep from * to end, working last sc into first ch on row 1.

Row 3 Make 3 knots, 1sc into next free knot along last row, * make 2 knots, 1sc into next free knot along last row, rep from * to end.

Rep row 3 throughout.

Bar and lattice

Materials Fine to medium-weight wool for a dressy effect; cotton or synthetic yarn for a cool look.
Uses Ribbon-threaded dress yoke or inset panel; all-over pattern for café curtain.

Make a number of ch divisible by 4 plus 1, 5ch, turn.
Row 1 1dc into 10th ch from hook, * 3ch, skip 3ch, 1dc into next ch, rep from * to end, 4ch, turn.
Row 2 * 1sc into 2nd of 3ch, 2ch, 1dc into dc, 2ch, rep from * to end, ending with 2sc into 2nd ch, 2ch, 1dc into t-ch, 5ch, turn.
Row 3 1dc into next dc, * 3ch, 1dc into next dc, rep from * to end, working last dc into t-ch, 4ch, turn.
Rep rows 2 and 3 throughout.

Star stitch

Materials Fine wool, silk crêpe or rayon for a soft, pretty look; medium-weight yarn, soft string or lurex for a rich textured effect.
Uses Dress inset panel or shawl border; all-over repeat for button-through cardigan, cushion set or bedspread border.

Make a number of ch divisible by 4 plus 1, 3ch, turn.
Row 1 1dc into 8th ch from hook, (1ch, 1dc) 3 times into same ch, *
* skip 3ch, 1dc into next ch, (1ch, 1dc) 3 times into same ch, rep from * to last 4ch, skip 3ch, 1dc into last ch, 3ch, turn.
Row 2 1dc into 2nd ch sp of shell, (1ch, 1dc) 3 times into same ch sp, rep from * to end, 1dc into t-ch, 3ch, turn.
Rep row 2 throughout.

Picot lace ground

Materials Medium-weight mohair for a winter wedding; silk or lurex for a special party look.

Uses All-over pattern for bride's lacy wrap; glittery triangular shawl, lacy cravat or beaded sash.

Make a number of ch divisible by 15 plus 1, 7ch, turn.

Row 1 1sc into 3rd ch from hook, – called picot – 2ch, skip 9ch, 1dc into next ch, * 5ch, pc, 2ch, skip 4ch, 1dc into next ch, rep from * to end, 8ch, pc, 2ch, turn.

Row 2 Skip first dc, 1dc into next dc, * 5ch, 1dc into next dc, (5ch, pc, 2ch, 1dc into next dc) twice, rep from * to last 2pc, 5ch, 1dc into next dc, 5ch, pc, 2ch, 1dc into 3rd ch beyond pc, 8ch, pc, 2ch, turn.

Row 3 Skip first dc, 1dc into next dc, *1dc into each of next 5ch, 1dc into next dc, (5ch, pc, 2ch, 1dc into next dc) twice, rep from * ending with 1dc into each of next 5ch, 1dc into next dc, 5ch, pc, 2ch, 1dc into 3rd ch beyond pc, 8ch, pc, 2ch, turn.

Row 4 Skip first dc, 1dc into next dc, *1dc into each of next 6dc, (5ch, pc, 2ch, 1dc into next dc) twice, rep from * ending with 1dc into each of next 6dc, 5ch, pc, 2ch, 1dc into 3rd ch beyond pc, 8ch, pc, 2ch, turn.

Row 5 Skip first dc, 1dc into next dc, * 5ch, pc, 2ch, skip 5dc, 1dc into next dc, (5ch, pc, 2ch, 1dc into next dc) twice, rep from * ending with 5ch, pc, 2ch, skip 5dc, 1 dc into next dc, 5ch, pc, 2ch, 1dc into 3rd ch beyond pc, 8ch, pc, 2ch, turn.

Row 6 Skip first dc, 1dc into next dc, * 5ch, pc, 2ch, 1dc into next dc, rep from * to end, working last dc into 3rd ch beyond pc, 8ch, pc, 2ch, turn.

Rep rows 2 to 6 throughout.

Ladder stitch

Materials Cotton for sunshine, lurex for moonlight; knitting worsted wool, mohair or angora for warmth.

Uses All-over pattern for beach wrap or blouson, cape or camisole top; jerkin, long, belted cardigan or scarf.

Make a number of ch divisible by 6 plus 1, 1ch, turn.

Row 1 1sc into 2nd ch from hook, * 5ch, skip 5ch, (1sc, 3ch, 1sc) into next ch, rep from * to last 6ch, 5ch, skip 5ch, 1sc into last ch, 1ch, turn.

Row 2 1sc into first sc, * 5ch, (1sc, 3ch, 1sc) into 5ch lp, rep from * to end, ending with 5ch, 1sc into last sc, 1ch, turn. Rep row 2 throughout.

Diamond stitch

Materials Perle cotton, synthetic yarn, slub linen or dishcloth cotton for easy care.

Uses Cushion border, bedcover flounce with added fringe or all-over repeat for lunch mat.

Make a number of ch divisible by 6 plus 1, 3ch, turn.

Row 1 2dc into 4th ch from hook, * 4ch, skip 5ch, 5dc into next ch, rep from * to last 6ch, 4ch, skip 5ch, 3dc into last ch, 1ch, turn.

Row 2 * (3dc, 3ch, 3dc) into 4ch sp, rep from * to end, 1sc into t-ch, 6ch, turn.

Row 3 * 5dc into 3ch sp, 4ch, rep from * to end, ending with 5dc into 3ch sp, 3ch, 1dc into t-ch, 5ch, turn.

Row 4 3dc into 3ch sp, * (3dc, 3ch, 3dc) into 4ch sp, rep from * to end, ending with (3dc, 2ch, 1dc) into t-ch, 3ch, turn.

Row 5 2dc into 2ch sp, * 4ch, 5dc into 3ch sp, rep from * to end, 4ch, 3dc into t-ch, 1ch, turn.

Rep rows 2 to 5 throughout.

Reseau stitch

Materials Silk, rayon or cotton yarn for summer wear; chunky or knitting worsted wool for warmth.

Uses Evening wrap or shawl inset panel; all-over repeat for blanket with contrast needle-weaving using fur strips or thick wool.

Make a number of ch divisible by 6 plus 1, 3ch, turn.

Row 1 1dc into 4th ch from hook, 1dc into next ch, * 3ch, skip 3ch, 1dc into each of next 3ch, rep from * to last 4ch, 3ch, skip 3ch, 1dc into last ch, 3ch, turn.

Row 2 2dc into first 3ch sp, * 3ch, 3dc into next 3ch sp, rep from * to end, ending with 3ch, 1dc into t-ch, 3ch, turn.

Rep row 2 throughout.

Irish net stitch

Materials Fine crochet cotton for a lacy look; medium-weight yarn for furnishing.

Uses All-over pattern for classic-style cardigan; combine with Irish motifs into all-over pattern for bedcover or buffet runner.

Make a number of ch divisible by 4 plus 1, 5ch, turn.

Row 1 (1sc, 3ch, 1sc) into 10th ch from hook, * 5ch, skip 3ch, (1sc, 3ch, 1sc) into next ch, rep from * to last 4ch, 5ch, skip 3ch, 1sc into last ch, 5ch, turn.

Row 2 (1sc, 3ch, 1sc) into 3rd of 5ch, 5ch, rep from * to end, 1sc into t-ch, 5ch, turn.

Rep row 2 throughout.

Crown stitch

Materials Soft cotton, silky crêpe or lurex for an extra pretty look; fine baby wool for lightness.

Uses Dress yoke or inset band; christening shawl inset border or all-over pattern for baby's carriage set.

Make a number of ch divisible by 7 plus 2, 2ch, turn.

Row 1 1hdc into 3rd ch from hook, 1hdc into next ch, * 3ch, skip 2ch, 1sc into next ch, 3ch, skip 2ch, 1hdc into each of next 2ch, rep from * to end, 2ch, turn.

Row 2 1hdc into each of first 2hdc, * 3ch, (1sc, 3ch, 1sc) into sc, 3ch, 1hdc into each of next 2hdc, rep from * to end, 1ch, turn.

Row 3 1sc into each of 2hdc, * 1sc into 3ch sp, 5ch, 1sc into next 3ch sp, 1sc into each of 2hdc, rep from * to end, 1ch, turn.

Row 4 1sc into each of first 2sc, * skip 1sc, 7sc into 5ch sp, skip 1sc, 1sc into each of next 2sc, rep from * to end, 2ch, turn.

Row 5 1hdc into each of first 2sc, * 3ch, skip 3sc, 1sc into next sc, 3ch, skip 3sc, 1hdc into each of next 2sc, rep from * to end, 2ch, turn.

Rep rows 2 to 5 throughout.

Peacock stitch

Materials Medium-weight cotton or acrylic for wash and wear; Shetland wool or mohair for lacy softness.

Uses Bedspread or curtain border; shawl inset panel, loose-fitting blouson top or scarf.

Make a number of ch divisible by 14 plus 1, 1ch, turn.

Row 1 1sc into 2nd ch from hook, * skip 6ch, 13 long dc into next ch (drawing lp up to $\frac{1}{2}$ in. to form a long dc), skip 6ch, 1sc into next ch, rep from * to end, 4ch, turn.

Row 2 1 long dc into sc, * 5ch, 1sc into 7th of 13 long dc, 5ch, 2 long dc into sc, rep from * to end, 1ch, turn.

Row 3 * 1sc bet 2 long dc, 13 long dc into sc, rep from * to end, 1sc bet long dc and t-ch, 4ch, turn. Rep rows 2 and 3 throughout.

Ruby lace ground

Materials Fine Shetland wool, cotton or synthetic yarn for a light lacy effect.

Uses Shawl inset panel, woven dress sleeve and bodice insertion or all-over pattern for bedcover border.

Make a number of ch divisible by 8, 1ch, turn.

Row 1 Starting into 2nd ch from hook * 1sc into next 4ch, 3ch, sl st into first of these 3ch – called picot – 1sc into each of next 4ch, turn, 9ch, sl st to first sc, turn, into the 9ch lp work 7sc, 3pc, 7sc, rep from * to end, 9ch, turn.

Row 2 * 1sc into 2nd of 3pc, 8ch, rep from * to end, 1sc into 2nd of 3pc, 4ch, 1dc, dc into t-ch, 1ch, turn.

Row 3 1sc into each of next 4ch, turn, 5ch, sl st to first sc, turn, 2pc, 7sc into 5ch lp, rep from * on first row to last 9ch, 1sc into each of next 4ch, turn, 5ch, sl st into first sc, turn, 7sc into 5ch lp, 2pc, turn.

Row 4 * 8ch, 1sc into 2nd of 3pc, rep from * to end, 3ch, turn.

Rep rows 1 to 4 throughout.

COLORWORK

*Patterns using two or more colors in a row
are easier to read if charted on graph paper (one square
equals one stitch). Read charts upwards from right-
hand corner. Bring second color yarn in by drawing
it through last two loops of first color, and vice
versa, keeping yarn not in use on wrong side (see p.12).*

Zigzags

Materials Chunky or knitting worsted yarn for warmth; medium-
weight cotton for sun wear.

Uses Kimono-style jacket or child's dressing gown inset panel; all-
over pattern for swimsuit, bikini or beach mat.

Repeat:
6 sts × 8 rows

Horizontal stripes

Materials Medium-weight yarn for a sporty finish; ½in. wide fabric strips for economy furnishing.

Uses All-over pattern for loose-fitting blazer or square-neck sweater; kitchen cushion or hearth rug.

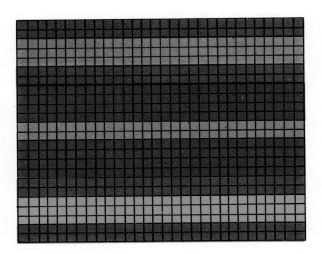

Repeat: 1 st × 24 rows

Vertical stripes

Materials 4-ply wool or novelty yarn for casual wear.
Uses Inset panel for mother and daughter button-through cardigan or man's waistcoat front; all-over repeat for patchwork blanket or scarf.

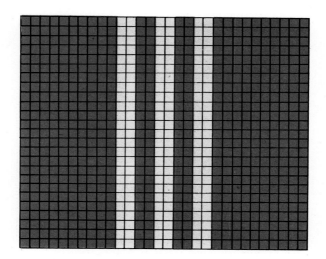

Repeat: 18 sts × 1 row

Diamonds

Materials Medium-weight wool or tweedy mix for snug warmth; cotton yarn for easy care.
Uses Father and son jacket inset panel, sweater band or bedroom slippers; bathroom set or shoulder bag border.

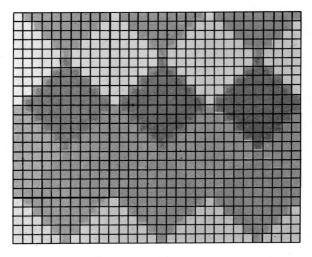

Repeat: 10 sts × 20 rows

PLAIN MEDALLIONS

Crochet is easily made into circles or squares by working in the round and increasing at regular intervals (see p.14). As each row is worked from the same side, there is no right or wrong side to the fabric. Medallion patterns may be plain, close-stitched, or a mixture of both.

Arcade diamond

Materials Fine wool for a lacy finish; random-dyed cotton for a softly mottled look.

Uses Join together for throwover bedspread or shawl; baby carrier, curtain or placemat.

Make 6ch and join into a ring with a sl st into first ch.

Round 1 3ch, 15dc into ring, join with a sl st to 3rd of first 3ch.

Round 2 5ch, * 1dc into next dc, 2ch, rep from * 14 times more, join with a sl st to 3rd of first 5ch.

Round 3 Sl st into first sp, 3ch, (1dc, 3ch, 2dc) into same sp, * (2ch, 1sc into next sp) 3 times, 2ch, (2dc, 3ch, 2dc) into next sp, rep from * twice more, (2ch, 1sc into next sp) 3 times, 2ch, join with a sl st to 3rd of first 3ch.

Round 4 Sl st into next 3ch sp, 3ch, (1dc, 3ch, 2dc) into same sp, * (2ch, 1sc into 2ch sp) 4 times, 2ch, (2dc, 3ch, 2dc) into 3ch sp, rep from * twice more, (2ch, 1sc into 2ch sp) 4 times, 2ch, join with a sl st to 3rd of first 3ch.

Round 5 Sl st into 3ch sp, 3ch, (2dc, 2ch, 3dc) into same sp, * (1ch, 2dc into 2ch sp) 5 times, 1ch, (3dc, 2ch, 3dc) into 3ch sp, rep from * twice more, (1ch, 2dc into 2ch sp) 5 times, 1ch, join with a sl st to 3rd of first 3ch. Fasten off.

Framed square

Materials Medium-weight yarn for warmth; jute and a jumbo hook for furnishing.

Uses Motif for potholder, coaster or all-over repeat for patchwork coverlet; casserole stand, or enlarge motif for doormat.

Make 8ch and join into a ring with a sl st into first ch.

Round 1 3ch, 15dc into ring, join with a sl st to 3rd of first 3ch.

Round 2 5ch, (1dc into next dc, 2ch) 15 times, join with a sl st to 3rd of first 5ch.

Round 3 Sl st into first 2ch sp, 3ch, 2dc into same sp, 1ch, * 3dc into next sp, 1ch, rep from * to end, join with a sl st to 3rd of first 3ch.

Round 4 Sl st into first ch sp, * (3ch, 1sc into next sp) 3 times, 6ch, 1sc into next sp, rep from * 3 times more, omitting last sc and join with a sl st to sl st at beg of rnd.

Round 5 Sl st into first 3ch sp, 3ch, 2dc into same sp, 3dc into each of next 2 3ch sps, * (5dc, 2ch, 5dc) into 6ch sp, 3dc into each of next 3 3ch sps, rep from * twice more, (5dc, 2ch, 5dc) into 6ch sp, join with a sl st to 3rd of first 3ch.

Round 6 3ch, 1dc into each dc to corner, * (1dc, 1tr, 1dc) into 2ch sp, 1dc into each dc to next corner, rep from * twice more, (1dc, 1tr, 1dc) into 2ch sp, 1dc into each dc to end, join with a sl st to 3rd of first 3ch.
Fasten off.

Primula circle

Materials Knitting worsted yarn for appliqué; very fine crochet cotton or silk for an extra special finish.

Uses Spot motif or posy pattern for sweater decoration; applied motif for wedding dress or veil, baby's christening gown or a lapel badge.

Make 4ch and join into a ring with a sl st into first ch.
Round 1 1ch, 11sc into ring, join with a sl st to first ch.
Round 2 1ch, 1sc into same place, inserting hook into back half of each st work 2sc into each st to end, join with a sl st to first ch.
Round 3 3ch, * skip 1sc, 1sc into back half of next sc, 2ch, rep from * to end, join with a sl st to first of first 3ch.

Round 4 Into each 2ch sp work 1sc, 1dc, 2tr, 1dc and 1 sc, join with a sl st to first sc.
Fasten off.

Scalloped circle

Materials Fine to medium-weight crêpe, rayon or cotton for a lacy look.

Uses Single motifs for applying to bridesmaid's ribbon sash or hairslide; all-over repeat for placemat, tablecloth or bedspread.

Make 6ch and join into a ring with a sl st into first ch.
Round 1 3ch, 23dc into ring, join with a sl st to 3rd of first 3ch.
Round 2 5ch, 1dc into sl st, 1ch, * skip 2dc, (1dc, 2ch, 1dc) into next dc, 1ch, rep from * 6 times more, join with a sl st to 3rd of first 5ch.
Round 3 Sl st into 2ch sp, 3ch, (1dc, 2ch, 2dc) into same sp, * 1sc into 1ch sp, (2dc, 2ch, 2dc) into 2ch sp, rep from * 6 times more, 1sc into 1ch sp, join with a sl st into 3rd of first 3ch.
Round 4 Sl st into 2ch sp, 3ch, (2dc, 1ch, 3dc) into same sp, * 1sc before next sc, 1sc after the same sc, (3dc, 1ch, 3dc) into 2ch sp, rep from * 6 times more, 1sc before next sc, 1sc after the same sc, join with a sl st to 3rd of first 3ch.
Fasten off.

Plain hexagon

Materials 4-ply wool, knitting worsted or acrylic yarn for light warmth; cotton or rayon yarn for wash and wear.

Uses Join medallions for plain or patchwork shawl, blanket, waist-coat or hot water-bottle cover; single motif for placemat or coaster.

Make 4ch and join into a ring with a sl st into first ch.
Round 1 1ch, 11sc into ring, join with a sl st to first ch, turn.
Round 2 2ch, * 3hdc into next sc, 1hdc into next sc, rep from * 4 times more, 3hdc into next sc, join with a sl st to 2nd of first 3ch, turn.
Round 3 2ch, 1hdc into next hdc, * 3hdc into next hdc, 1hdc into each of next 3hdc, rep from * 4 times more, 3hdc into next hdc, 1hdc into next hdc, join with

a sl st to 2nd of first 2ch, turn.
Round 4 2ch, 1hdc into each of next 2hdc, * 3hdc into next hdc, 1hdc into each of next 5hdc, rep from * 4 times more, 3hdc into next hdc, 1hdc into each of next 2hdc, join with a sl st to 2nd of first 2ch, turn.
Cont in this way, working 2 more hdc along each side in each rnd until hexagon is the required size. Fasten off.

Spiral hexagon

Materials Medium-weight yarn or space-dyed cotton for town wear; fine string for a country look.

Uses Beret, bedspread and bolster module, or scatter cushion; drawstring bag base or hot pot stand.

Make 5ch and join into a ring with a sl st into first ch.

Round 1 * 6ch, 1sc into ring, rep from * 5 times more, sl st over first 3ch of first lp.

Round 2 * 4ch, 1sc into 6ch lp, rep from * 5 times more, working last sc into sl st before the first 4ch.

Round 3 * 4ch, 2sc into 4ch lp, 1sc into sc, rep from * 5 times more, working last sc into last sc at end of last rnd.

Round 4 * 4ch, 2sc into 4ch lp, 1sc into each of next 2sc, rep from * to end.

Round 5 * 4ch, 2sc into 4ch lp, 1sc into each of next 3sc, rep from * to end.

Cont in this way, working 1 more sc in each group on each rnd until motif is the required size, ending with a sl st into next sc. Fasten off.

Flower hexagon

Materials Medium-weight yarn for country furnishing; raffia for cottage kitchen wear.

Uses Patchwork blanket module or pillow panel; cooking pot stand or placemat.

Make 6ch and join into a ring with a sl st into first ch.

Round 1 4ch, (1dc into ring, 1ch) 11 times, join with a sl st to 3rd of first 4ch.

Round 2 3ch, 2dc into sp, 1dc into dc, 2ch, * 1dc into dc, 2dc into sp, 1dc into dc, 2ch, rep from * 4 times more, join with a sl st to 3rd of first 3ch.

Round 3 3ch, 1dc into same place, 1dc into each of next 2dc, 2dc into next dc, 2ch, * 2dc into next dc, 1dc into each of next 2dc, 2dc into next dc, 2ch, rep from * 4 times more, join with a sl st to 3rd of first 3ch.

Round 4 3ch, 1 dc into same place, 1dc into each of next 4dc, 2dc into next dc, 2ch, * 2dc into next dc, 1dc into each of next 4dc, 2dc into next dc, 2ch, rep from * 4 times more, join with a sl st to 3rd of first 3ch.

Round 5 3ch, 1dc into each of next 7dc, * 3ch, 1sc into 2ch sp, 3ch, 1dc into each of next 8dc, rep from * 4 times more, 3ch, 1sc into 2ch sp, 3ch, join with sl st to 3rd of first 3ch.

Round 6 Sl st into next dc, 3ch, 1dc into each of next 5dc, * 3ch, (1sc into 3ch sp, 3ch) twice, skip next dc, 1dc into each of next 6dc, rep from * 4 times more, 3ch, (1sc into 3ch sp, 3ch) twice, join with a sl st to 3rd of first 3ch.

Round 7 Sl st into next dc, 3ch, 1dc into each of next 3dc, * 3dc, (1sc into 3ch sp, 3ch) 3 times, 1dc into each of next 4dc, rep from * 4 times more, 3ch, (1sc into 3ch sp, 3ch) 3 times, join with a sl st to 3rd of first 3ch.

Round 8 Sl st between 2nd and 3rd dc of group, 3ch, 1dc into same place, * 3ch, (1sc into 3ch sp, 3ch) 4 times, 2dc between 2nd and 3rd dc of grp, rep from * 4 times more, 3ch, (1sc into 3ch sp, 3ch) 4 times, join with a sl st to 3rd of first 3ch.

Round 9 Sl st into 3ch sp, 3ch, 3dc into same sp, (4dc into 3ch sp) 4 times, * 3ch, skip 2dc, (4dc into 3ch sp) 5 times, rep from * 4 times more, 3ch, join with a sl st to 3rd of first 3ch. Fasten off.

LACE MEDALLIONS

By working chains and large spaces into a decorative motif, lacy medallions are quickly and easily made. Alternatively, separate motifs can be made and the lace mesh background worked around them. Lace medallion patterns include both stylized and natural forms, geometric designs and cobwebby net grounds. Insert medallions singly or join together to form a border, panel or all-over repeat.

Willow lace square

Materials Fine cotton, rayon or silky yarn for a pretty lace look.
Uses All-over square or diamond repeat for shawl, tablecloth, buffet runner or throwover lampshade cover.

Make 5ch and join into a ring with a sl st into first ch.
Round 1 1ch, 11sc into ring, sl st to first ch.
Round 2 * 15ch, sl st into next sc, rep from * 11 times more; working last sl st into sl st at end of rnd 1.
Round 3 Sl st along to center of first lp, * 4ch, 1sc into next lp, 4ch, (yo, insert hook into next lp, yo, draw lp through, yo, draw through 2 lps) 3 times, yo, draw through all 4 lps on hook – called cluster – 4ch, cl into same lp, 4ch, 1sc into next lp, rep from * 3 times more, working last sc into sl st at beg of rnd.
Round 4 Sl st along to center of first 4ch lp, 3ch, cl into this same lp, * 4ch, 1sc into next lp, 4ch, (cl, 4ch, cl) into next lp, 4ch, 1sc into next lp, 4ch, cl into next lp, rep from * 3 times more, but omit last cl and sl st to 3rd of first 3ch.
Fasten off.

59

Irish lace square

Materials Fine to medium-weight rayon, cotton or lurex for an overall lacy effect.

Uses All-over repeat for bedcover, window pelmet, cushion panel or shimmery evening jacket.

Make 16ch.

Round 1 1sc into first of the 16ch, to make a lp, (15ch, 1sc into same ch as before) twice, 3 lps now made.

Round 2 24sc into each lp, join with a sl st to first dc.

Round 3 1sc into each sc all around, join with a sl st to first sc.

Round 4 Sl st into each of next 3sc, * 1sc into next sc, ** 4ch, 1sc into 3rd ch from hook, 5ch, 1sc into 3rd ch from hook, 1ch ** – called 1 picot loop – skip 4sc, 1sc into next sc, (1 picot loop, skip 4sc, 1sc into next sc) twice, 1 picot lp, 1sc into 5th sc of next leaf, rep from * twice more, omitting the last sc and working a sl st into first sc of rnd. 12 picot lps now made.

Round 5 Sl st along to center of first picot lp, * 8ch, 1sc into center of next lp, turn, sl st into lp just made, 3ch, 9dc into same lp, 1dc into next sc, turn, 4ch, skip first 2dc, 1dc into next dc, (1ch, skip 1dc, 1dc into next dc) 3 times, 1ch, skip 1dc, 1dc into 3rd of 3ch, 4ch, 1sc into 3rd ch from hook, 2ch, 1sc into same lp, (1 picot lp, 1sc into center of next lp) twice, rep from * 3 times more, but omitting last sc and working a sl st into sl st at base of first 8ch.

Round 6 Sl st up side of dc and into each of next 3ch, * 1 picot lp, 1dc into center 1ch sp, 1 picot lp, 1sc into last dc of "crown" (1 picot lp, 1sc into center of next lp) twice, 1 picot lp, 1sc into 3rd of 3ch at beg of "crown" rep from * 3 times more, omitting last sc and working a sl st into sl st before first picot lp.

Round 7 Sl st along to center of first picot lp, work as rnd 5, but working 4 picot lps between each "crown" instead of 2.

Round 8 As rnd 6 but working 2 more picot lps along each side of square.

Fasten off.

COLOR MEDALLIONS

*With one or two exceptions color medallions
are worked in the round where each new color
is joined at the beginning of a round (see p.12). Many
small medallions can be made from yarn oddments and
joined in an all-over repeat, or at random, into a large
multi-color blanket, rug or bedspread. Other
medallions, such as America and Alpine squares
may be increased into cushion or rug sizes
simply by adding more rows in color sequence.*

Ridged square

Materials Chunky, knitting worsted or synthetic yarn for a warm, lacy effect; wool oddments for cost cutting.
Uses Border for knitted afghan or woven shawl; all-over pattern for blanket or cushion.

This square uses 5 colors, A, B, C, D and E.
Using A, make 8ch and join into a ring with a sl st.
Round 1 4ch, 3tr into ring, ★ 5ch, 4tr into ring, rep from ★ twice more, 5ch, join with a sl st to 4th of first 4ch.
Fasten off.

Make 3 more squares in the same way, one each in B, C and D.
Using E, join squares thus: place 2 squares tog with wrong sides tog, join E to 1 corner, work 3sc into sp, 1sc bet each tr, 3sc into sp. Fasten off.

Wheel square

Materials Knitting worsted, mohair or bouclé yarn for a tweedy look; random-dyed for a mottled effect.

Uses Waistcoat inset panel or blanket square; all-over design for a baby's hooded cape or cot cover.

This uses 2 colors, A and B.
Using A, make 8ch and join into a ring with a sl st into first ch.

Round 1 Using A, 6ch, * 1dc into ring, 3ch, rep from * times more, join with a sl st to 3rd of first 6ch. Break off A.

Round 2 Join B to any sp, 3ch, 3dc into same sp, * 2ch, 4dc into next sp, rep from * 6 times more, 2ch, join with a sl st to 3rd of first 3ch. Break off B.

Round 3 Join A to any sp, 3ch, 5dc into same sp, * 1ch, 6dc into next sp, 3ch, 6dc into next sp, rep from * twice more, 1ch, 6dc into next sp, 3ch, join with a sl st to 3rd of first 3ch. Break off A.

Round 4 Join B to a 1ch sp, * 3ch, 1sc between 3rd and 4th dc of grp, 3ch, (2dc, 3ch, 2dc) into 3ch sp, 3ch, 1sc bet 3rd and 4th dc of grp, 3ch, 1sc into 1ch sp, rep from * 3 times more, omitting last sc and join with a sl st to first ch.
Fasten off.

Begonia square

Materials Chunky or knitting worsted wool for warmth; medium-weight cotton or synthetic yarn for light furnishing.
Uses All-over patchwork repeat for poncho or coverlet; café curtain, room divider or stepped-edge table cover.

This uses 2 colors, A and B.
Using A, make 4ch and join into a ring with a sl st into first ch.
Round 1 Using A, 4ch, ** yo twice, insert hook into ring, yo, draw lp through, (yo, draw through 2 lps) twice ** rep from ** to ** 3 times more, yo, draw through 5 lps, * 4ch, rep from ** to ** 5 times, yo, draw through 6 lps, rep from * 6 times more, 4ch, join with a sl st to 4th of first 4ch. Break off A.
Round 2 Join B to a 4ch lp, 3ch, 3dc into same sp, * 4dc into next sp, 6ch, 4dc into next sp, rep from * twice more, 4dc into next sp, 6ch, join with a sl st to 3rd of first 3ch.
Fasten off.

Star hexagon

Materials Chunky wool for bedsitter furnishing.
Uses All-over pattern for patchwork blanket and cushion set.

This motif uses 3 colors, A, B and C.
Using A, make 6ch and join into a ring with a sl st into first ch.
Round 1 4ch, 2tr into ring, ★ 1ch, 3tr into ring, rep from ★ 4 times more, 1ch, join with a sl st to 4th of first 4ch, turn.
Round 2 Using A, ★ 1sc into 1ch sp, 7ch, rep from ★ 5 times more, join with a sl st to first sc. Break off A.
Round 3 Join B to a 7ch lp, into each lp work 1hdc, 2dc, 3tr, 2dc, 1hdc, join with a sl st to first hdc. Break off B.
Round 4 Join C to first hdc of a petal, 4ch, 1dc into each of 2dc, 1hdc into each of 3hdc, 1dc into each of 2dc, 1tr into hdc, ★ 1tr into hdc, 1dc into each of 2dc, 1hdc into each of 3tr, 1dc into each of 2dc, 1tr into hdc, rep from ★ 4 times more, join with a sl st to 4th of first 4ch.
Fasten off.

American square

Materials Chunky yarn for country-style furnishing; 4-ply novelty mix, bouclé or mohair for budget fashion.

Uses All-over patchwork repeat for fringed rug, bedspread or pillow; poncho, triangular shawl or waistcoat inset panel.

This square uses 2 colors, A and B.

Using A, make 6ch and join into a ring with a sl st into first ch.

Round 1 Using A, 3ch, 2dc into ring, ★ 3ch, 3dc into ring, rep from ★ twice more, 3ch, join with a sl st to 3rd of first 3ch. Break off A.

Round 2 Join B to any sp, 3ch, (2dc, 3ch, 3dc) into same sp, ★ 1ch, (3dc, 3ch, 3dc) into next sp, rep from ★ twice more, 1ch, join with a sl st to 3rd of first 3ch. Break off B.

Round 3 Join A to a 3ch sp, 3ch, (2dc, 3ch, 3dc) into same sp, ★ 1ch, 3dc into 1ch sp, 1ch, (3dc, 3ch, 3dc) into 3ch sp, rep from ★ twice more, 1ch, 3dc into 1ch sp, 1ch, join with a sl st to 3rd of first 3ch. Break off A.

Round 4 Join B to a 3ch sp, 3ch, (2dc, 3ch, 3dc) into same sp, ★ (1ch, 3dc into 1ch sp) twice, 1ch, (3dc, 3ch, 3dc) into 3ch sp, rep from ★ twice more, (1ch, 3dc into 1ch sp) twice, 1ch, join with a sl st to 3rd of first 3ch. Fasten off.

Mosaic octagon

Materials Very fine crochet cotton, silk or lurex for extra delicate finery; medium-weight cotton or acrylic yarn for furnishing.
Uses Border detail for wedding veil or spot repeat for net dress; placemat or pot holder motif or all-over design for octagonal tablecloth.

This uses 2 colors, A and B.
Using A, make 6ch and join into a ring with a sl st into first ch.
Round 1 Using A, 3ch, 15dc into ring, join with a sl st to 3rd of first 3ch. Break off A.
Round 2 Join B to any dc, 3ch, (1dc, 1ch, 2dc) into same place, ★ skip 1dc, (2dc, 1ch, 2dc) into next dc, rep from ★ 6 times more, join with a sl st to 3rd of first 3ch. Break off B.

Round 3 Join A to a 1ch sp, 3ch, (1dc, 1ch, 2dc) into same sp, ★ 1dc bet grp, (2dc, 1ch, 2dc) into 1ch sp, rep from ★ 6 times more, 1dc bet grp, join with a sl st to 3rd of first 3ch. Break off A.
Round 4 Join B to any st, 1ch, 1sc into each st all around, join with a sl st to first ch.
Fasten off.

Tricolor square

Materials Lightly twisted 4-ply yarn for extra softness; pastel shades for baby wear.

Uses All-over pattern for bright afghan blanket or full-length hooded coat and scarf; pram cover or baby carrier.

This square uses 3 colors, A, B and C.

Using A, make 8ch and join into a ring with a sl st into first ch.

Round 1 Using A, 4ch, 5tr into ring, ★ 3ch, 6tr into ring, rep from ★ twice more, 3ch, join with a sl st to 4th of first 4ch.

Round 2 Using A, 5ch, ★★ yo twice, insert hook into next tr, yo, draw lp through, (yo, draw through 2 lps) twice, ★★ rep from ★★ to ★★ into each of next 4tr, yo, draw through 6 lps, ★ 5ch, 1 sl st into 2nd of 3ch, 5ch, rep from ★★ to ★★ into each of next 6tr, yo, draw through 7 lps, rep from ★ twice more, 5ch, 1 sl st into 2nd of 3ch. Break off A.

Round 3 Join B to top of a cl, ★ work (3tr, 1ch, 3tr, 2ch, 3tr, 1ch, 3tr) into 3ch sp of rnd 1, 1 sl st into top of next cl, rep from ★ 3 times more, working last sl st into same place as yarn was joined, and joining A at the same time Break off B.

Round 4 Using A, 4ch, 5tr into same sl st, ★ (6tr, 2ch, 6tr) into 2ch sp, 6tr into sl st at top of next cl, rep from ★ twice more, (6tr, 2ch, 6tr) into 2ch sp, join with a sl st to 4th of first 4ch. Break off A.

Round 5 Join C to last sl st of rnd 4, 1ch, 1sc into each of next 5tr, 1dc into 1ch sp between grp of tr on rnd 3, ★ 1sc into each of next 6tr, 3sc into 2ch sp at corner, (1sc into each of next 6tr, 1dc into 1ch sp bet grp of tr on rnd 3) twice, rep from ★ twice more, 1sc into each of next 6tr, 3sc into 2ch sp at corner, 1sc into each of next 6tr, 1dc into 1ch sp bet grp of tr on rnd 3, join with a sl st to first ch.

Round 6 Using C, 3ch, 1dc into each st all around, working 3dc into center st of each corner, end by joining with a sl st to 3rd of first 3ch.

Fasten off.

Lotus circle

Materials Medium-weight wool or synthetic mix for snug warmth; dishcloth string for easy care.

Uses Join in patchwork pattern for throwover bedspread, cushion set or beret; single motif for pot holder or bag base.

This motif uses 2 colors, A and B.

Make 3ch in A and join into a ring with a sl st into first ch.

Round 1 1ch, 7sc into ring, join with a sl st to first ch.

Round 2 1ch, join B and work 1sc into same place, * 1sc in A and 1sc in B into next st, rep from * to end, join with a sl st in A into first ch.

Round 3 1ch, working into the back half only of each st on *every* rnd, 2sc in B into next sc, 1sc in A next sc, rep from * to last st, 2sc in B into last st, join with a sl st in A into first ch.

Round 4 1ch, * 2sc in B into next sc, 1sc in B into next sc, 1sc in A into next sc, rep from * to last 2 sts, 2sc in B into next sc, 1sc in B into next sc, join with a sl st in A to first ch.

Round 5 1ch, * 2sc in B into next sc, 1sc in B into each of next 2sc, 1sc in A into next sc, rep from * to last 3 sts, 2sc in B into next sc,

1sc in B into each of next 2sc, join with a sl st in A into first ch.

Cont in this way, working 1 more st in B in each grp on every rnd until there are 8 sts in B in each grp (63sts in the rnd).

Round 10 1 ch, * 2sc in A into next sc, 1sc in B into each of next 7sc, 1sc in A into next sc; rep from * to end, but omit the last sc in A and join with a sl st in A into first ch.

Round 11 1ch, * 2sc in A into next sc, * 1sc in A into each of next 2sc, 1sc in B into each of next 6sc, 1sc in A into next sc, rep from * to end, but omit the last sc in A and join with a sl st in A into first ch.

Cont in this way, still inc 7 sts in every rnd, but working 1 st less in B in each grp on every rnd until only 1 st in B remains (112 sts in the rnd).

Fasten off.

Alpen square

Materials Medium-weight yarn oddments for economy; space-dyed 4-ply or acrylic yarn for a soft, shaded effect.
Uses Combine with contrast repeat for bedspread, jerkin or poncho; all-over pattern for hooded baby carrier or cot cover.

This square uses 4 colors, A, B, C and D.
Using A, make 6ch and join into a ring with a sl st into first ch.
Round 1 Using A, 1ch, 15sc into ring, join with a sl st to first ch.
Round 2 Using A, 11ch, ★ skip 3sc, 1sc into next sc, 10ch, rep from ★ twice more, join with a sl st to first of first 11ch.
Round 3 Using A, 1ch, ★ 11sc into 10ch lp, 1sc into sc, rep from ★ 3 times more, but omit last sc and join with a sl st to first ch. Break off A.

Round 4 Join B to 6th of 11sc, 1ch, 1sc into same place, 1sc into each sc all around and 1sc, 1ch, 1sc into each corner, join with a sl st to first ch. Break off B.
Round 5 Join C to corner and work as rnd 4. Break off C.
Round 6 Join D to corner and work as rnd 4. Break off D.
Cont in the same way, working 1 rnd in C, then 2 rnds in A.
Fasten off.

Two-tone hexagon

Materials Chunky yarn oddments for budget brightness; a jumbo hook and fine rope or sisal for cottage-style furnishing.
Uses All-over repeat for hexagonal sofa blanket, cushion set or cape; enlarged motif for doormat or kitchen rug.

This motif uses 2 colors, A and B.
Using A, make 6ch and join into a ring with a sl st into first ch.
Round 1 Using A, 3ch, 2dc into ring, * 3ch, 3dc into ring, rep from * 4 times more, 3ch, join with a sl st to 3rd of first 3ch. Break off A.
Round 2 Join B to 13ch sp, 5ch, (2dtr, 2ch, 3dtr) into same sp, * (3dtr, 2ch, 3dtr) into next sp, rep from * 4 times more, join with a sl st to 5th of first 5ch. Break off B.
Round 3 Join A to same place as sl st, 3ch, 1dc into each of next 2dtr, * (2dc, 2ch, 2dc) into 2ch sp, 1dc into each of next 6dtr, rep from * 4 times more, (2dc, 2ch, 2dc) into 2ch sp, 1dc into each of next 3dtr, join with a sl st to 3rd of first 3ch. Break off A.
Round 4 Join B into any st, 3ch, 1dc into previous st, * skip 1 st, 1dc into next st, 1dc into the skipped st, rep from * all around, join with a sl st to 3rd of first 3ch. Fasten off.

RELIEF MOTIFS

Three-dimensional medallions are made by using the bobble or embossed technique (see p.11), or by working twice into the same round. Motifs range from tiny flowers to large geometric patterns. Apply medallions singly or join in an all-over repeat.

Looped nosegay

Materials Medium-weight cotton or fine wool for a deep pile effect.
Uses Combine with contrast patterns into blanket square, cushion set or wall panel decoration.

This medallion uses 3 colors, A, B and C.
Using A, make 3ch and join into a ring with a sl st into first ch.
Round 1 1ch, 3sc into ring, sl st into first ch.
Round 2 1ch, 1sc into same place, 2sc into each sc to end, sl st into first ch.
Round 3 As rnd 2. Break off A.
Round 4 Join B, 1ch, * 2sc into next sc, 1sc into next sc, rep from * 7 times more, but omit last sc and work a sl st into first ch. Break off B.
Round 5 Join C, 1ch, * 2sc into next sc, 1sc into each of next 2sc, rep from * 7 times more, but omit last sc and work a sl st into first ch.

Round 6 Using C, 1ch, * 2sc into next sc, 1sc into each of next 3sc, rep from * 7 times more, ending as before. Break off C.
Round 7 Turn work and join A with wrong side facing, 1ch, * yo, insert hook into next st, hold a pencil behind work and take the yarn round it to form a loop, yo, draw lp through, yo, draw through 3 lps on hook, rep from * to end, sl st to first ch. Break off A.
Round 8 Join B and work as rnd 7, but inc 8 sts evenly in the round. Break off B.
Round 9 Join C and work as rnd 8. Fasten off.

Magnolia

Materials Soft, loosely twisted cotton, rayon or fine wool for a three-dimensional finish.

Uses Spot repeat for sweater, party dress border, haircomb trim, bedroom cushion set or guest towel posy motif.

This medallion uses 3 colors, A, B and C.

Using A, make 5ch and join into a ring with a sl st into first ch.

Round 1 1ch, 4sc into ring, sl st to first ch.

Round 2 1ch, 1sc into same place, 2sc into each sc to end, sl st to first ch.

Round 3 2ch, 1hdc into same place, 2hdc into each sc to end, sl st to 2nd of first 2ch.

Round 4 Inserting hook into front strand only of each st, * 3ch, 1tr into same place, 2tr into each of next 2hdc, (1tr, 3ch, 1 sl st) into next hdc, 1 sl st into next hdc, rep from * 4 times more. Break off A.

Round 5 Join B behind the center of one petal, then inserting hook into back strand only of each st of rnd 4, work as rnd 4 but working dtr instead of tr. Break off B.

Round 6 Join C in *front* of work into a sc of rnd 1, (3ch, 1sc into next sc) 4 times, 3ch, sl st into same place as join. Fasten off.

Cineraria

Materials Fine crochet cotton, linen thread or rayon mix for a firm textured effect.

Uses Spot repeat for counterpane squares and matching bolster or hat brim decoration.

Make 8ch and join into a ring with a sl st into first ch.

Round 1 3ch, 17dc into ring, sl st into 3rd of 3ch.

Round 2 8ch, (1dc into next dc, 5ch) 17 times, sl st into 3rd of first 8ch.

Round 3 ★ 1sc into each of next 2ch, (1sc, 1ch, 1sc) into next ch, 1sc into each of next 2ch, skip 1dc, rep from ★ 17 times more.

Round 4 ★ 1sc into each of next 3sc, (1sc, 1ch, 1sc) into 1ch sp, 1sc into each of next 3sc, rep from ★ 17 times more.

Rounds 5, 6, 7, 8 and 9 As rnd 4, working one more sc in each grp on each round.

Round 10 ★ 5ch, 1sc bet 8th and 9th of next 16sc (i.e., above the dc which was skipped in rnd 3) rep from ★ 16 times more, 5ch, sl st into base of first 5ch.

Round 11 ★ 5ch, 1sc into 3rd ch of lp, 5ch, 1sc into next sc, rep from ★ 17 times more; omitting last sc and working a sl st into base of first 5ch.

Round 12 Sl st along to 3rd ch of lp, ★ 5ch, 1sc into next lp, rep from ★ 35 times more, omitting last sc and working a sl st into sl st before first 5ch.

Round 13 As rnd 12. Fasten off.

Bobble square

Materials Medium-weight cotton or rayon, plain or random-dyed acrylic or synthetic mix for wash and wear.

Uses Single or multi-colored patchwork blanket, shawl, bath-mat, bedroom rug, linen bag or tabard.

Make 12ch and join into a ring with a sl st into first ch.

Round 1 3ch, 1dc into ring * (yo, insert hook into ring, yo, draw lp through, yo, draw through 2 lps) 6 times, yo, draw through 6 lps, yo, draw through rem 2 lps – called bobble – 4dc into ring, rep from * twice more, bobble, 2dc into ring, sl st to 3rd of first 3ch.

Round 2 3ch, 1dc into same place, * 1dc into each of next 3 sts, 2dc into next dc, 1ch, 2dc into next dc, rep from * 3 times more, but omit the last 2dc and sl st to 3rd of first 3ch.

Round 3 3ch, 1 dc into same place, * (1 dc into next dc, bobble into next dc) twice, 1dc into next dc, 2dc into next dc, 2ch, 2dc into next dc, rep from * 3 times more, but omit the last 2dc and sl st to 3rd of first 3ch.

Round 4 3ch, 1dc into same place, * 1dc into each of next 7 sts, 2dc into next dc, 3ch, 2dc into next dc, rep from * 3 times more, but omit last 2dc and sl st into 3rd of first 3ch.

Round 5 3ch, 1dc into same place, * 1dc into each of next 2dc, (bobble into next dc, 1dc into next dc) 3 times, 1dc into next dc, 2dc into next dc, 4ch, 2dc into next dc, rep from * 3 times more, but omit last 2dc and sl st to 3rd of first 3ch.

Round 6 3ch, 1dc into same place * 1dc into each of next 11 sts, 2dc into next dc, 4ch, 2dc into next dc, rep from * 3 times more, but omit last 2dc and sl st to 3rd of first 3ch.
Fasten off.

Flower square

Materials Medium-weight wool, silky yarn or crochet cotton for a deep sculptured effect.

Uses All-over repeat for cushion or lacy bedspread center panel, hot water-bottle cover or padded teacosy.

Make 4ch and join into a ring with a sl st into first ch.

Round 1 * 2ch, 4dc into ring, sl st into ring, rep from * 3 times more.

Round 2 Sl st into back of 3rd dc, * keeping yarn at back of work, 4ch, sl st into back of 3rd dc of next grp, rep from * twice more, 4ch, join with a sl st to first sl st.

Round 3 Into each lp work 1 sl st, 5dc, 1 sl st.

Round 4 * 6ch, 1 sl st into back of sl st between petals, rep from * 3 times more.

Round 5 3ch, (2dc, 3ch, 3dc) into same lp, *1ch, (3dc, 3ch, 3dc) into next lp, rep from * twice more, 1ch, join with a sl st to 3rd of first 3ch.

Round 6 3ch, (2dc, 3ch, 3dc) into same sp, * 1ch, 3dc into 1ch sp, 1ch, (3dc, 3ch, 3dc) into 3ch sp, rep from * twice more, 1ch, 3dc into 1ch sp, 1ch, join with a sl st to 3rd of first 3ch.

Round 7 3ch, (2dc, 3ch, 3dc) into same sp, * (1ch, 3dc into 1ch sp) twice, 1ch, (3dc, 3ch, 3dc) into 3ch sp, rep from * twice more, (1ch, 3dc into 1ch sp) twice, 1ch, join with a sl st to 3rd of first 3ch.
Fasten off.

Dandelion

Materials Light-weight wool, slub linen or cotton yarn for an embossed effect.

Uses Appliqué motif (with embroidered stalks) for cardigan pocket or sweater front; straw hat-brim trim or lapel badge.

Make 4ch and join into a ring with a sl st into first ch.
Round 1 1ch, 11sc into ring, sl st to first ch.
Round 2 Working into front half only of each sc, work (1sc, 4ch, 1sc) into each sc.

Round 3 Working into back half only of each sc of rnd 1, * 6ch, (1sc, 6ch, 1sc) into next sc, rep from * to end.
Fasten off.

RELIEF MEDALLIONS

Greater depth is given to fine crochet motifs
by working over one or more additional threads and then
working single crochet over this foundation. Relief
motifs may either be incorporated into a simple net
background – as a border or as an all-over repeat –
or applied individually as a fashion accessory.

Spray of leaves

Materials Fine crochet cotton, linen thread, silk or lurex for well-shaped motifs.

Uses Cardigan pocket or sweater motif, or combine with all-over lacy stitch for cushion, shawl or bedspread.

For first leaf make 16ch.

Row 1 1sc into 2nd ch from hook, 1sc into each of next 13ch, 3sc into next ch, cont along other side of foundation ch, 1sc into each of next 14ch, 1ch, turn.

Row 2 Working throughout into the back half only of each st, 1sc into each of next 11sc, 1ch, turn.

Row 3 1sc into each of next 11sc, 3sc into next st, 1sc into each of next 12sc, 1ch, turn.

Row 4 1sc into each of next 12sc, 3sc into next sc, 1sc into each of next 10sc, 1ch, turn.

Row 5 1sc into each of next 10sc, 3sc into next sc, 1sc into each of next 10sc, 1ch, turn.

Row 6 1sc into each of next 10sc, 3sc into next sc, 1sc into each of next 8sc, 1ch, turn.

Row 7 1sc into each of next 8sc, 3sc into next sc, 1sc into each of next 8sc, 1ch, turn.

Row 8 1sc into each of next 8sc, 3sc into next sc, 1sc into each of next 6sc.

Fasten off.

Make 2 more leaves in the same way.

For stalk make 30ch, sl st into base of one leaf, 8ch, sl st into base of second leaf, turn; working over 3 strands of yarn work 1sc into each ch to end, turn, sl st into each of first 30 sts, then sl st to base of third leaf (this will now be opposite to the first leaf).

Fasten off.

Rose

Materials Very fine crochet cotton, silk or linen thread for forming tiny delicate flowers.

Uses Spot appliqué for party cardigan, pearl-centred buttons, wide hat-brim decoration on hanging ribbons, drawstring fob ends, haircomb or hairslide trim.

Wind the yarn 3 or 4 times around a finger, remove the loop from finger and fasten with a sl st.

Round 1 1ch, 17sc into ring, sl st to first ch.

Round 2 6ch, skip 2sc, 1hdc into next sc, * 4ch, skip 2sc, 1hdc into next sc, rep from * 3 times more, 4ch, sl st into 2nd of first 4ch.

Round 3 Into each 4ch lp work (1sc, 1hdc, 3dc, 1hdc, 1sc), end with a sl st into first sc.

Round 4 Sl st into back of hdc on rnd 2, * 5ch, keeping yarn at back of work 1 sl st into back of next hdc on rnd 2, rep from * 4 times more, 5ch, sl st into same hdc as first sl st.

Round 5 Into each 5ch lp work (1sc, 1hdc, 5dc, 1hdc, 1sc), end with a sl st to first sc.

Round 6 Sl st into back of sl st on rnd 4, * 6ch, keeping yarn at back of work 1 sl st into next sl st on rnd 4, rep from * to end.

Round 7 Into each 6ch lp work (1sc, 1hdc, 7dc, 1hdc, 1sc), end with a sl st into first sc. Fasten off.

Four leaf clover

Materials Fine wool, silky yarn, metallic thread or crochet cotton for a delicate look.

Uses Single motif for lapel accessory, draped party dress neck or jacket trim, or link with lacy pattern for bedcover.

Make 5ch and join into a ring with a sl st into first ch.

Round 1 1ch, 13sc into ring, sl st to first ch.

Round 2 1ch, 1sc into next sc, * 4ch, ** yo twice, insert hook into next st, yo, draw lp through, (yo, draw through 2 lps) twice ** rep from ** to ** twice more into same st, yo, draw through 4 lps on hook, 3ch, 1sc into each of next 2sc, rep from * 3 times more, make 6ch for stalk, turn and work 1 sl st into each ch, then 1 sl st into next sc on flower. Fasten off.

Hibiscus

Materials Very fine cotton, rayon, silk or metallic thread for a detailed flower effect.
Uses Random appliqué pattern for sheer fabric dress or evening wrap, sash trim for dress bodice, mock buttons, or link with lacy pattern for shawl or throwover.

This medallion uses 2 colors, A and B.
Using A, make 6ch and join into a ring with a sl st into first ch.
Round 1 3ch, 19dc into ring, sl st to 3rd of 3ch. Break off A.
Round 2 Join B, * 1ch, 1dc into next dc, 2dc into next dc, 1dc into next dc, 1ch, 1sc into next dc, rep from * 4 times more, but omit last sc and work a sl st into same place as join.
Fasten off.
Cut a few strands of each color and join to back of work to form stalk.

Shamrock

Materials Fine crochet cotton, silk or rayon for a raised effect.
Uses Appliqué motif for bride's veil, sweater or cushion; combine with lacy pattern for table linen border.

Make 16ch.
Round 1 1sc into first of the 16ch, to make 1 lp, (15ch, 1sc into same ch as before) twice (3 lps now made).
Round 2 Lay a length of yarn along the work, then working over this thread, work 22sc into each 15ch lp, sl st into first sc.
Round 3 Working over length of yarn, skip 1sc, * 1sc into each of next 20sc, skip 2sc (1sc of this lp and 1sc of next lp) rep from * twice, sl st into first sc, 25ch, turn.
Stalk 1sc into 2nd ch from hook, then over length of yarn work 1sc into each ch, then work 1 sl st into first sc of shamrock.
Fasten off.

AFGHAN CROCHET

Also known as Tunisian stitch, this draws on the techniques of both knitting and crochet. A long hooked needle is used and the work differs from crochet in several ways; no turning chains are required and the rows are worked in pairs without turning the work (see p.13). Afghan stitches generally produce a closely-woven fabric.

Afghan stitch

Materials Medium-weight synthetic yarn or knitting worsted wool for a dense texture and warmth; crochet cotton, silk or rayon for a cool firm fabric.

Uses All-over pattern for father and son jerkin and matching cap; mother and daughter waistcoat front, shoulder bag or floor cushion inset panel.

Make a foundation row of 20ch.
Row 1 Working from R to L, miss first ch, insert hook into 2nd ch from hook, yo and draw through 1 loop, ★ insert hook into next ch, yo and draw through 1 loop, rep from ★ to end of ch length keeping all loops on hook.
Row 2 Working from L to R, yo and draw through first 2 loops on hook, ★ yo and draw through next 2 loops on hook, rep from ★ to end leaving 1 loop on hook.
Row 3 Working from R to L, miss first vertical loop on RS of fabric, ★ insert hook from R to L into next vertical loop, yo and draw through 1 loop, rep from ★ to end keeping all loops on hook.
Row 4 Work as row 2.
Repeat rows 3 and 4 throughout.

Fan stitch

Materials Medium-weight yarn for a nubbly texture; baby wool for softness.

Uses Mother and daughter cardigan inset panel or all-over repeat for loose slipover; bedjacket, baby's dress or shawl border.

Make a no. of ch with a multiple of 3 sts plus 1 extra.

Work 3 rows in plain Afghan stitch, (see p.87).

Row 4 Yo and draw through first loop, ★ 2ch, yo and draw through the loop on hook and the next 3 loops, rep from ★ to end.

Row 5 1ch, ★ insert hook into each of next 2ch and draw up a loop, insert hook into the vertical loops of the 3 sts which were worked tog and draw up a loop, rep from ★ to end, working into the last 2ch, then into the vertical loop of the end st.

Row 6 Work the sts off in pairs in the usual way.

Queen lace stitch

Materials 4-ply wool, acrylic or cotton yarn for a classic look; random-dyed yarn for a gently mottled effect.

Uses Dress bodice or all-over pattern for slipover, classic-style cardigan or hat; baby's coat, bonnet or cot blanket.

Make an even no. of ch and work first 2 rows in plain Afghan stitch, (see p.87).

Row 3 ★ Lay yarn across front of work, insert hook from right to left in front of first 2 sts tog, yo and draw lp through purlwise, insert hook between sts, yo and draw lp through, rep from ★ to last st, insert hook into last st, yo, draw lp through.

Row 4 As row 2.

Rep rows 3 and 4 throughout.

Color squares

Materials Silk, rayon, cotton or crêpe yarn for a soft luxurious effect; knitting worsted, bouclé wool or tweedy mix for wintry days.

Uses All-over repeat for long evening jacket or long fringed silky scarf; man's sweater or waistcoat inset panel or all-over pattern for child's double-breasted jacket and matching cap.

This pattern uses 2 colors, A and B.
Make a no. of ch divisible by 8.
Row 1 Using A, insert hook into 2nd ch, yo, draw lp through, (insert hook into next ch, yo, draw lp through) twice; using B, (insert hook into next ch, yo, draw lp through) 4 times, cont in this way working 4 lps in A and 4 lps in B.

Row 2 Using B, yo, draw through one lp, (yo, draw through 2 lps) 3 times, using A, (yo, draw through 2 lps) 4 times, cont in this way to end.
Cont in this way, work 4 more rows, then alternate the colors and work 6 rows.
Rep these 12 rows throughout.

Brocade stitch

Materials Shetland, knitting worsted, crêpe wool or acrylic mix for warmth and wear.

Uses All-over pattern for ski sweater and matching hat, shoulder bag, slipper socks, blanket panel or travel rug.

This pattern uses 2 colors, A and B.
Using A, make a no. of ch divisible by 10, plus 2.
Work first 2 rows of plain Afghan stitch, (see p.87).
Row 3 Using B, insert hook into first lp without drawing yarn through – called 1 sl st – * work 2 plain sts, (yo, insert hook into next st, draw lp through, yo, draw through 2 lps – called tr st –) 4 times, 2 plain sts, 2 sl sts rep from * to end.
Row 4 Using B, as row 2.
Rows 5 and 6 Using A, as plain afghan stitch.
Row 7 Using B, 2 tr sts, * 2 plain sts, 2 sl sts, 2 plain sts, 4 tr sts, rep from * to end.
Row 8 Using B, as row 2.
Rep these 8 rows throughout.

Narcissus lace stitch

Materials Medium-weight wool, crêpe or synthetic yarn for a lacy look.

Uses Dress yoke or inset panel; all-over design for baggy T-shirt, bedjacket or shawl border.

Make a no. of ch divisible by 4, and work first row in plain Afghan stitch, (see p.87).

Row 2 Yo, draw through 2 lps, ★ 4ch, yo, draw through 5 lps, rep from ★ until 3 lps rem on hook, 3ch, yo, draw through 3 lps, 1ch.

Row 3 Insert hook into first ch, yo, draw lp through, rep into each of next 2ch, ★ (insert hook into next ch, yo and draw lp through) 4 times, rep from ★ to end.

Rep rows 2 and 3 throughout, ending with row 2.

EDGINGS

This group of stitch patterns offers one of the most versatile ranges of stitch decoration, texture and uses. Applied edgings need not be restricted to crocheted articles, but may be quite successfully applied to hand or machine knitting, or to woven fabric. All the stitch patterns illustrated may be used as edgings but can easily be made into double-edged trim by repeating the pattern in the opposite side of the foundation row. It is a good idea to wash cotton trim before applying to prevent any shrinking pulling the article out of shape.

Piranesi edging

Materials Fine rayon or crochet cotton for a pretty look.
Uses Trim for print nightie and matching négligé, petticoat, lower edge of woven fabric overblouse or guest towel set.

Make 8ch and join into a ring with a sl st into first ch.
Row 1 3ch, 8dc into ring, turn.
Row 2 4ch, 1dc into 2nd dc, ★ 1ch, 1tr into next dc, rep from ★ 5 times more, 1ch, 1dc into 3rd of 3ch.
Row 3 5ch, 1dc into 2nd dc, ★ 2ch, 1dc into next dc, rep from ★ 5 times more, 2ch, 1dc into 3rd of 4ch.
Row 4 6ch, 1dc into 2nd dc, ★ 3ch, 1dc into next dc, rep from ★ 5 times more, 3ch, 1dc into 3rd of 5ch.
Row 5 ★ (1sc, 3dc, 1sc) into 3ch sp, rep from ★ 7 times more, 8ch, turn and sl st into 2nd of first 3dc, turn.
Row 6 3ch, 8dc into 8ch lp, turn.
Row 7 4ch, 1dc into 2nd dc, ★ 1ch, 1dc into next dc, rep from ★ 5 times more, 1ch, 1dc into 3rd of 3ch, sl st into 2nd dc of next group of 3, turn.
Row 8 5ch, miss first dc, 1dc into next dc work as row 3 from ★ to end.
Row 9 Work as row 4, then sl st into 2nd dc of next group of 3, turn.
Rep rows 5 to 9 for the length reqd, then work row 5, omitting the 8ch at end of row.
Heading
Working along straight edge of work, 5ch, 1dc into next row-end, ★ 2ch, 1dc into next row-end, rep from ★ to end, turn.
Next row 3ch, ★ 2dc into 2ch sp, 1dc into next dc, rep from ★ to end, working last dc into 3rd of 5ch.
Fasten off.

Picot arch edging

Materials Fine cotton or rayon yarn for household trim.
Uses Finish for bedlinen, bedside tablecover, net curtain or pretty kitchen shelf edging.

Make a ch the length reqd, having a no. of ch divisible by 3 plus 1, 2ch, turn.
Row 1 1dc into 4th ch from hook, 1dc into each ch to end.
Row 2 ★ 3ch, skip next 2dc, 1dc into next dc, rep from ★ to end.

Row 3 Sl st into first lp, ★ 6ch, sl st into 4th ch from hook, 2ch, 1sc into next lp, rep from ★ to end. Fasten off.

Nugget edging

Materials Fine to medium-weight wool, cotton, lurex or synthetic yarn for a delicate finish.
Uses Sweater or bolero trim, silk scarf edging or straw hat band with added flowers.

Make a ch the length reqd, having a no. of ch divisible by 8 plus 3, 2ch, turn.
Row 1 1dc into 4th ch from hook, 1dc into each ch to end.
Row 2 3ch, 1dc into each of next 2dc, ★ (2ch, miss 2dc, 1dc into next dc) twice, 1dc into each of next 2dc, rep from ★ to end, working last dc into t-ch.
Row 3 4ch, leave lp of each on hook work 3tr into next sp, yo, draw through all 4 lps on hook, ★ 9ch, leaving last lp of each on

hook work 3tr into next sp, then 3tr into next sp after the 3dc, yo, draw through all 7 lps on hook, rep from ★ to end, ending with 9 ch, work a 3dc cluster into last sp, 1dc in to t-ch.
Row 4 Sl st into top of first cluster, work (1sc, 1hdc, 7dc, 1hdc, 1sc) into each 9ch lp, sl st into top of last cluster. Fasten off.

Triangle edging

Materials Very fine cotton, linen or silk thread for the tiniest border trim.

Uses Finish for baby clothes, handkerchiefs and hems, greetings card or picture mount.

Make a ch the length reqd, having a no. of ch divisible by 4 plus 1, 2ch, turn.

Row 1 1dc into 4th ch from hook, 1dc into each ch to end.

Row 2 3ch, 3dc into first dc (edge st), * skip 3dc, 1sc into next dc, 3ch, 3dc into same dc, rep from * to end, ending with skip 3dc, 1sc into t-ch.

Fasten off.

Fan edging

Materials Medium-weight crêpe, rayon, lurex or crochet cotton for a bold trim; fine cotton or silk for a delicate finish.

Uses Lower edges of slinky evening dress and jacket or curtain tieback; circular table cover or cushion trim.

Make 10ch and join into a ring with a sl st into first ch.

Row 1 3ch, 14dc into ring, 5ch, turn.

Row 2 Skip first 2dc, (1dc into next dc, 2ch, skip 1dc) 6 times, 1dc into 3rd of 3ch, 3ch, turn.

Row 3 * 7dc into next sp, take hook out of lp, insert it into 3rd of 3ch, then into the lp and draw lp through – called popcorn st – 3ch, rep from * 5 times more, 1 popcorn st into last sp, 10ch, turn.

Row 4 Skip first 2 sps, (1sc, 5ch, 1sc) into next sp, 3ch, turn.

Row 5 13dc into 5ch lp, 1sc into 10ch lp, 5ch, turn.

Row 6 Skip sc and first dc, (1dc into next dc, 2ch, skip 1dc) 6 times, 1dc into 3rd of 3ch, 3ch, turn.

Rep rows 3 to 6 for the length reqd, ending with a 3rd row. Do not turn or break off yarn.

Heading

1dc into sp below last popcorn st, * 5ch, 1dc into 10ch lp, 5ch, 1dc into sp below next popcorn st, rep from * to end.

Fasten off.

Scallop edging

Materials Plain or random-dyed rayon, silk or synthetic yarn for a firm, pretty edging.
Uses Edging for knitted or crocheted cardigan or bedjacket; pillow, petticoat or carriage cover trim.

Worked into a row of sc on edge of work, having a multiple of 6sc plus 1.

1 sl st into first sc, * skip 2sc, 5dc into next sc, skip 2sc, 1 sl st into next sc, rep from * to end.

Richelieu edging

Materials Medium-weight rayon, lurex or cotton yarn for soft furnishing.
Uses Trim for lampshade, roller blind, cushion set or lower edge of upholstered furniture.

Make a ch the length required, having a number of ch divisible by 7 plus 1, 2ch, turn.
Row 1 1dc into 4th ch from hook, 1dc into each ch to end.
Row 2 * 6ch, skip 6dc, 1sc into next dc, rep from * to end.
Row 3 Sl st into first lp, 3ch, (3dc, 2ch, 4dc) into same lp, * (4dc, 2ch, 4dc) into next lp, rep from * to end.
Row 4 * 3ch, 1sc into 2ch sp, (15ch, 1sc into same sp) 3 times, 3ch, 1sc between groups of dc, rep from * to end, working last sc into 3rd of 3ch at beg of row 3.

Row 5 8ch, * 3sc into first 15ch lp, (3dc, 2ch, 3dc) into next p, 3sc into next lp, rep from * to end.
Row 6 * 3ch, (3dc, 2ch, 3dc) into 2ch sp, 3ch, 1sc bet groups of sc, rep from * to end, working last sc into 8th of 8ch.
Row 7 * 3ch, (3dc, 2ch, 3dc, 2ch, dc) into 2ch sp, 3ch, 1sc into sc, rep from * to end, omit last sc and end with a sl st into first of 3ch. Fasten off.

Rose edging

Materials Fine crochet cotton, rayon or silky yarn for a light summery look.

Uses Light fabric dress neck and sleeve edge trim, lingerie or bedroom lampshade.

First motif
Make 8ch and join into a ring with a sl st into first ch.
Round 1 1ch, 11sc into ring, sl st to first ch.
Round 2 * 5ch, skip 1sc, 1sc into next sc, rep from * 4 times more, 5ch, 1sc into sl st at end of rnd 1.
Round 3 Into each 5ch lp work 1dc, 1hdc, 5dc, 1hdc and 1sc.
Round 4 Keeping hook behind petals just worked, work 1sc into first sc on rnd 2, * 4ch, 1sc into 3rd ch from hook – called picot – 5ch, pc, 2ch, 1sc into sc on rnd 2 bet next 2 petals, rep from * all around, ending with 1 sl st into first sc.
Fasten off.

Second motif
Work as given for first motif until the 4 rnds have been completed, but do not break off yarn. To join motifs, work in rows as follows:
Row 1 Sl st along to center of next pc lp, 1sc into same lp, 4ch, pc, 5ch, pc, 2ch – called picot loop – 1sc into center of next pc lp, turn.
Row 2 1 pc lp, 1sc into center of next pc lp, 1 pc lp, 1sc into sc at base of pc lp on previous row, turn.

Row 3 Sl st to center of next pc lp, 1sc into same lp, 1 pc lp, 1sc into center of next pc lp, turn.
Row 4 4ch, pc, 1ch, sl st into center any lp on first motif, 3ch, pc, 2ch, 1sc into next pc lp on 2nd motif, 3ch, pc, 2ch, 1sc into sc at base of previous row.
Fasten off.
Make as many motifs as reqd, joining each as shown, leaving one pc lp free at each side of join.

Heading
With right side facing join yarn to pc lp at top of first motif, 1sc into same place as join, * (5ch, 1dc into next pc lp) 4 times, 5ch, 1so into next pc lp, rep from * to end.
Fasten off.

Scalloped edge
With right side of other edge facing join yarn to loop before the top lp of first motif, 5ch, pc, 3ch, * into next lp (at top of motif) work (1tr, 3ch, 1sc into top of tr) 6 times, then 1tr, 5ch, 1sc into pc lp at join of motifs, 1 pc lp, 1sc into next lp, 5ch, rep from * along edge, ending with tr grp as before, 5ch, pc, 2ch, 1sc into next pc lp.
Fasten off.

Elm edging

Materials Medium-weight cotton or rayon for a leafy finish.
Uses Roller blind or towel trim; trolley cloth or table cover.

First leaf
Make 16ch.
Row 1 1sc into 2nd ch from hook and into each of next 13ch, 3sc into last ch, cont along the other side of ch, 1sc into each ch to end, 2sc into same ch as first sc, turn.
From here, work always into the back half only of each st.
Row 2 1sc into each of next 13sc, 1ch, turn.
Row 3 1sc into each sc, 3sc into center ds of gr of 3sc, 1sc into each sc along other side to 1sc before next 3sc gr, 1ch, turn.
Row 4 1sc into each sc to 3rd sc from end, working 3sc into center sc of 3sc gr, 1ch, turn.
Rows 5, 6 and 7 As row 4.
Row 8 1sc into each sc to center of 3sc gr, sl st into center sc. Fasten off.
Second leaf
Work as for first leaf until 7 rows have been completed, 1ch, turn.

Row 8 1 sl st into corresponding sc on first leaf, 1sc into each sc to center of 3sc gr, sl st into center sc. Fasten off.
Make as many leaves as reqd, joining each as shown.
Heading
Row 1 Join yarn to center sc of first leaf, 1sc into same place, * 7ch, keeping the last lp of each on hook, work 1tr into center sc along side of this leaf, then 1tr into center sc along side of next leaf, yo and draw through all 3 lps on hook, called a joint tr – 7ch, 1sc into center sc at top of this leaf, rep from * to end, 4ch, turn.
Row 2 * (skip 1ch, 1dc into next ch, 1ch) 3 times, miss 1ch, 1dc into top of joint dc, 1ch, (skip 1ch, 1dc into next ch, 1ch) 3 times, miss 1ch, 1dc into sc, rep from * to end.
Fasten off.

Bouquet edging

Materials Light-weight crochet cotton or random-dyed rayon for a deep lacy trim.

Uses Border for triangular shawl, filet-net café curtain or throwover bedspread.

Make 21ch.
Row 1 1dc into 8th ch from hook, (2ch, skip 2ch, 1dc into next ch) 3 times, 5ch, skip 3ch, (1dc, 3ch) 3 times into next ch, 1dc into same ch, 1ch, turn.
Row 2 (1sc, 1hdc, 1dc, 1tr, 1dc, 1hdc, 1sc) into each of 3 3ch sps – shamrock made – 5ch, 1dc into 5ch lp, (2ch, 1dc into next dc) 4 times, 2ch, skip 2ch, 1dc into next ch, 5ch, turn.
Row 3 Skip first dc, 1dc into next dc, (2ch, 1dc into next dc) 4 times, 2ch, 1dc into 5ch lp, 7ch, (1dc, 3ch) 3 times into tr in center of 2nd petal, 1dc into same place, 1ch, turn.

Row 4 Make a shamrock as before, 5ch, 1dc into 7ch lp, ★ 2ch, 1dc into next dc, rep from ★ to end, working last dc into 3rd of 5ch, 5ch, turn.
Row 5 As row 3 but working (2ch, 1dc into next dc) 6 times instead of 4 times.
Row 6 As row 4.
Row 7 Skip first dc, 1dc into next dc, (2ch, 1dc into next dc) 3 times, 7ch, skip 4 sps, (1dc, 3ch) 3 times into next sp, 1dc into same sp, 1ch, turn.
Rep rows 2 to 7 for length reqd, ending with a 6th row.
Fasten off.

Sunflower edging

Materials Fine rayon, synthetic yarn or crochet cotton for a pretty decorative finish.

Uses Roller blind or window pelmet trim, bedlinen or buffet runner border; curtain tie back.

First motif
Wind yarn about 10 times around one finger, then sl loop off finger.

Round 1 Work 40sc into ring, sl st to first sc.

Round 2 1ch, 1sc into each sc to end, sl st to first ch.

Round 3 As rnd 2.

Round 4 * 5ch, skip 1sc, 1sc into next sc, rep from * to end, working last sc into sl st at end of rnd 3 (20 lps).

Round 5 Sl st into first lp, 4ch, leaving last lp of each on hook, work 2 tr into same lp, yo, draw through all 3 lps on hook, * 5ch, leavin the last lp of each on hook, work 3tr into next lp, yo, draw through all 4 lps on hook, rep from * to end, 5ch, sl st to top of first cluster.
Fasten off.

Second motif
Work as for first motif until 4 rnds have been completed.

Round 5 Sl st into first lp, 4ch, work a 2tr cluster as on first motif, * 2ch, sl st into a 5ch lp on first motif, 2ch, work a 3tr cluster into next lp on 2nd motif, rep from * twice more, then complete as for first motif.

Make as many motifs as reqd, joining each in the same way. Leave 7 lps free at top and bottom of motifs between the 3 lps joining the motifs.

Heading
With right side facing join yarn to 7th lp before join on first motif, 9ch, 1tr into next lp, * (4ch, 1sc into next lp) 3 times, 4ch, 1tr into next lp, 4ch, leaving the last lp of each on hook work 1dtr into next lp and 1dtr into first free lp on next motif, yo, draw through all 3 lps on hook, 4ch, 1tr into next lp, rep from * to last motif, (4ch, 1sc into next lp) 3 times, 4ch, 1dtr into next lp, 4ch, 1dtr into next lp, 7ch, turn.

Next row * 1dc into tr, (4ch, 1dc into sc) 3 times, 4ch, 1dc into tr, 4ch, 1dc into joined dtr, 4ch, rep from * to end, working last dc into 5th of 9ch.
Fasten off.

Index

Acknowledgments

Contributors
Janet Swift

Assistants
Maggie Elliott
Gilly Squires

Artist
John Hutchinson

Photographers
Ian O'Leary
Steve Oliver

Typesetting
Contact Graphics Ltd

Reproduction
F. E. Burman Ltd